Seriously

The Teenagers A-Z Guide to Radical Christianity

By Neil O'Boyle

Copyright © 2003 Neil O'Boyle

First Published in 2003 by Authentic Lifestyle

09 08 07 06 05 04 03   7 6 5 4 3 2 1
Authentic Lifestyle is an imprint of Authentic Media
PO Box 300, Carlisle, Cumbria, CA3 0QS, UK
and PO Box 1047, Waynesboro, GA 30830-2047, USA
www.paternoster-publishing.com

The right of Neil O'Boyle to be identified as the Author of
this Work has been asserted by them in accordance with
Copyright, Designs and Patents Act 1988

All rights reserved. No part of this publication may be
reproduced, stored in a retrieval system, or transmitted by
any means, electronic, mechanical, photocopying,
recording or otherwise, without the prior permission of the
publisher or a licence permitting restricted copying. n the
UK such licences are issued by the Copyright Licensing
Agency, 90 Tottenham Court Road, London, W1P 9HE

British Library Cataloguing in Publication Data

A catalogue record for this book is available from
the British Library

ISBN 1-85078-446-9

Cover design by Paul Lewis
Internal layout and illustrations by Greg Riddle
Typeset by Temple Design
Printed in Great Britain by Cox and Wyman, Reading

Contents

Warning!	5
Age	7
Bad Language	15
Church	23
Drink, Drugs and Cigarettes	29
Encouragement	39
Forgiveness	45
Guilt	51
Honesty	57
Identity	63
Judging	69
Kindness	77
Love	83
Money	91
Needs	99
Obedience	107
Parents	115
Quiet Time	123
Relationships	129
Sex	137
Temptation	147
Understanding	155
Videos	163
Witnessing	173
eXcellent worship!	181
You've Got It	189
Zits, weight and all that stuff	197

Warning!

Do not read this book without first looking below.

If you are sick of just playing it cool, if you are frustrated by the fact that you aren't being challenged in your faith, if you are desperate to move closer to Jesus, in other words if you want a radical Christianity, then this book is definitely for you!

Every action you take, every area of your life, will come under close examination as you turn the pages. What are your relationships like? How good are you at managing your money? Do you hold grudges, drink a little too much, twist the truth from time to time, want more from your boy or girlfriend, struggle in your quiet times? Are you quick to jump to conclusions? Do you wonder who you are and what you're doing? Then get ready for the ride of your life!

This book expects you to join in, in fact unless you do then you won't be challenged at all. If you really want to be stretched and move closer to being a different person – one who is radically sold out for Jesus – then don't hold back! Answer the questions, think through the issues, step into other people's shoes and be honest at every stage.

If, however, you are happy as you are, don't need any challenges and certainly don't want any questions asked then I suggest you put this book down or give it away. You don't need it, because it is only for those who are ready to get as serious as they possibly can with Jesus.

You have been warned.

Age

The big issue

Jenny was fourteen years old; she was bright, outgoing and attractive. However she always felt inferior next to her older sister Sarah who was eighteen, had finished her A-levels and would soon be heading off to university. As far as Jenny was concerned, Sarah had everything in life. She could do whatever she liked, see who she wanted and come home as late as she wanted. Pubs, 18-certificate movies, nightclubs, a serious boyfriend, great eating places, an incredible wardrobe of clothes – you name it, Sarah did it (or had it) and as Jenny saw it, if Sarah didn't do it, it wasn't worth doing.

Jenny was tired of always being the little sister who had to be home by 9 and in bed at 10 each week night, while Sarah was out on the town. This was crazy! She was fed up always being told to get off the phone and finish her homework. She pretty much viewed it that the only time she got to live was in her dreams.

One Friday evening Jenny and a couple of her friends decided they were going to live a little. She was allowed out until ten-thirty on Fridays and Saturdays. At ten o'clock she opened the door and screamed, 'I'm home and I'm going upstairs to bed!' then she closed the door behind her and stepped out into the street, leaving her parents assuming she was now safely at home. She met her friends, each of whom had spent what must have been hours in front of the mirror to look as drop dead gorgeous as possible. Jenny was wearing her sister's clothes and could easily have passed for eighteen. The night began well. They all made it into the local nightclub and had no problem getting served. Then things took a turn for the worse – they became increasingly drunk and just as they were about to leave, the club was raided by the police. Jenny was taken back to the police station, cautioned for underage drinking and made to wait until her confused and subdued parents arrived to take her home!

Talking point

- Do you think Jenny was right to feel inferior because she was the younger sister?
- If you were Sarah, how would you feel towards Jenny trying to be like you and to do things that you do?
- Have you ever felt in any way like Jenny?
- What would you have done differently if you had been Jenny?
- Below are some of the reasons why young people would rather be older than they are. Do you agree/disagree? What would you add?

Bible point

1 Timothy 4:12 *'So don't let anyone look down on you because you are young, but set an example for the believers in speech, in life, in love, in faith and in purity'*
Lots of people look down on teenagers just because they happen to be younger. Timothy was looked down on and the apostle Paul wrote to encourage him not to let it bother him and to rise above it. Take Paul's advice – amaze people by being a fantastic example in what you say and how you act, just like Timothy did.

1 Samuel 16:7 *'The Lord does not look at the things man looks at. Man looks at the outward appearance, but the Lord looks at the heart'*
When Israel needed a king, God sent a prophet named Samuel to the house of a man with many sons. Here's a quick peek at a conversation that developed between Samuel and Jesse (the father). 1 Sam 16:11-13, 'Are these all the sons you have?' (asked Samuel) 'There is still the youngest but he is tending the sheep' Jesse replied. 'So he sent for him (he was called David) and had him brought in ... Then the Lord said (to Samuel) "Rise and anoint him; he is the one!" David wasn't very old when he was chosen as the next King. But he became the finest King that Israel has ever had. He wasn't chosen because of how tall, strong, clever, good looking he was, nor because of his age but because of what God could see in his heart! If God wants you to do something, He won't let a small thing like your date of birth get in the way.

Luke 2:52 – *'Jesus grew in wisdom (mental) and stature (physical) and in favour with both God (spiritual) and man (social).'*
The only picture of Jesus as a teenager is here in this chapter in Luke's gospel. Is there something that we can learn from the story? It tells us

that Jesus grew mentally, physically, spiritually and socially. That he was balanced and well developed. 'Urh?' It means that his life wasn't chaotic. He didn't spend all of his day either in bed, on the computer or at McDonald's. It's important to grasp that your age and your growth go together, so be sure to have balance. Work hard at studying, exercise, make friends and take time to pray.

Listening point

'Grow up!', 'Act your age', 'Be responsible', 'Stop being childish.' Ever had anyone say that to you? It jars on you and makes you feel sick, doesn't it? It doesn't matter whether you are 13 or 30 – from time to time you're going to hear it. Someone is trying to insult you by saying that and whoever it is they are likely to be older, slamming you with their put down! It's the ace of statements, there is nothing you can say in reply. For if you retaliate you look immature and therefore merit the remark, if you don't reply then by default they come away triumphant! If you are a teenager, then welcome to a crazy world, people expect you to act like a so-called adult (whatever that actually means), but they don't give you the responsibility that goes with it. They want you to be mature but won't let you do all the really fun things in life because you're not old enough yet! Now is that confusing? You can't see certain films, sex is out of the question (if you are under sixteen[1]), you can't drive until your seventeen, you can't drink in public until you're eighteen.[2] In fact almost everything really worth doing in life has an age restriction tagged onto it. So why should you act like a responsible adult if you don't get any of the perks?

Can you remember your first ever real crush? The time when at the age of ten or eleven you asked the most drop-dead-gorgeous girl or boy in your class to marry you? The person of your dreams when you're ten, before you're officially a teenager, is hardly likely to be the person you settle down with in a life-long marriage, right? Fortunately common sense tells us that it would be a dumb move, regardless of the fact that it's illegal. Anyone knows a ten-year-old isn't ready for marriage – the very thought makes you feel kind of weird. People need to live a lot, mature a lot and grow a lot! A ten-year-old just isn't old enough! Even though you're far from being ten or eleven, plenty of the restrictions that you are faced with may seem unfair or unreasonable and in some of the cases you are probably right. But in other cases these restrictions are protecting you from making the mistakes that people older and not as bright as you make all the time. Getting drunk, watching horrific movies, having sex may not be what you want to do, especially as a Christian, but the fact that someone has said you can't because you're not mature enough may feel as enjoyable as a gigantic wart on your nose. You're left feeling you want to do stuff you shouldn't just for the kick of going against the so called wise guy (parent/teacher) who only ever says 'No' to anything and everything! But if you really want to do what's right, your only option is to treat the 'wart' with humility by accepting it, respecting it, and living with it until it drops off with age!

Every teenager at some point or other wants to be older than they actually are, like Jenny who wanted to be like her older sister. Nobody wants to be viewed as a baby who needs someone constantly looking over their shoulder the whole time. No matter where you are in your teens you're usually wishing you were at least two years older than you actually are right now. Very likely you have friends or brothers and sisters who are out there doing what you want to do and you feel their age offers credibility and the licence to freedom. Just think about it, if you're fifteen you can't drive yet, and if you're nineteen you can't get into the 21-restricted pubs and nightclubs, but you may be hanging around with people who can. It's frustrating and it's painful. But don't be too quick to rush time away, there are great benefits to being young. You are almost certainly going to be fitter, better looking and mentally sharper than most people fifteen or more years older than you. You are still climbing the hill while others are going down the other side. You have an entire life to live, a chance to bring about amazing dreams while others are running out of time with fewer plans available.

You may not have found this attempt at encouragement very comforting, and to add to the list of frustrations we have identified there are a few more, mainly related to that over-rated word 'hormones'. Hormones have a lot to do with the fact that teenage emotions are more like a roller-coaster ride than a smooth cruise on the river. One minute you're excited about something, the next you're fed up, you're in love then out of love, jealous, confident, confused, insecure; it can be a total nightmare! Just as you're trying to get to grips with the ride and the nausea is wearing off, it's usually then that some insensitive geek shoots the line, 'Grow up and act your age!' As the rage begins to rise, put a lid on it and walk away; these people just aren't worth it!

How you feel emotionally is a major part of your existence as a teenager, but try not to make things harder for yourself. Like Jesus is described in Luke 2:52, we need balance. We need to make sure we are not cramming our lives with all the wrong stuff, otherwise we will develop in a pretty odd way. Protect yourself and make sure you're as healthy as you can be in each area of your life. Balance brings maturity to every part of you. Jenny was too young to do the things her older sister did, she wasn't ready for it. Be quite sure that you are ready for the things you or your mates *think* it's cool to do, but – even more important – be sure God is happy with you doing them. Seek out balance for your life and soon enough the comments and head-banging insults will slow down.

Regardless of how old you are, don't make the mistake Jenny made, don't try to be someone or something you are not. Don't let others make you feel small or unimportant because of your age. Jesus said not to worry about tomorrow for tomorrow will worry about itself (Matthew 6:34). In other words, live for today. To God how old you are isn't important, because throughout the Bible God uses young people almost as much as adults. We've already looked at David and Timothy, but there were other characters who shook the world for God. Samuel was just a kid when God started talking to him, revealing the future to him and preparing him for a mighty career. Jeremiah was very young when he started out preaching the most radical messages – he was God's mouthpiece. Mary was probably no older than fourteen when the angel told her she would give birth to the Son of God! The disciples weren't exactly old guys either, they were most likely young enthusiastic teenagers who went on to change the world as we know today. Are you getting the picture yet? If you want to be used by God then your youth may be an advantage. Live your life and *expect* God to take hold of you in ways that will astonish other people. Remember, 'Don't let anyone look down on you because you are young'. Rise above it and live the full life that God has in mind for you *today* – whatever age you are (John 10:10).

Radical Action Guide

1. Be yourself and don't pretend to be anything or anyone you are not.
2. Then enjoy the things you want to do and don't feel guilty about it.
3. Be an example to anyone older than you by the way you live your life.
4. Be confident about who you are and not how old you are.
5. Take your value from God and not from your age.

---

[1] See chapter on Love

[2] See chapter on Drink, Drugs and cigarettes.

Balance of Age
the

1) In the inner core place a percentage of how much time and attention you give to each of the areas.

2) Within the outer circle, evaluate the areas of your life strengths for each segment of your life:
e.g. physical - fit etc
(See table below for more examples)

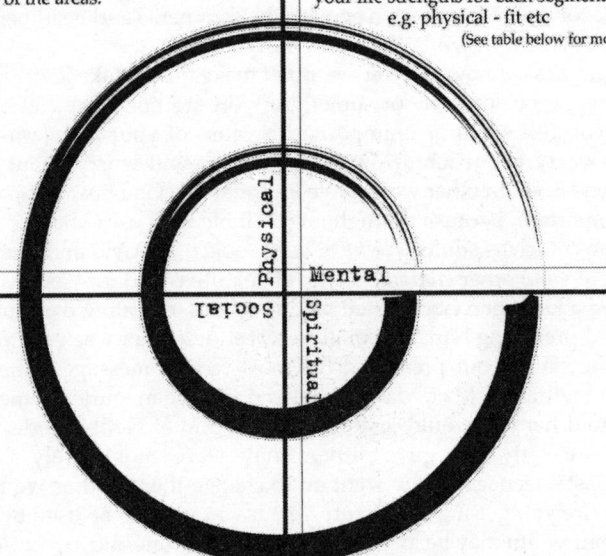

3) Outside the outer circle evaluate where there are weaknesses in each segment of your life.

4) Based on your answers, where do you need to make changes in your life to find the correct balance for your age and development?

For Physical, look for things like:	Size, height, fitness, athletic, general health
For Mental, look for things like:	General performance, Artistic & Creative, Preference for figures & formulae, enjoyment of study, sharp or plodder
For Social, look for things like:	Preference for group or singular friendships, close or distant friendships, Boy/Girlfriends, interests outside school
For Spiritual, look for things like:	Questioning deep issues like life & death, interest in God, Church, prayer & Bible reading, sensitivity about life and people

Think it through...

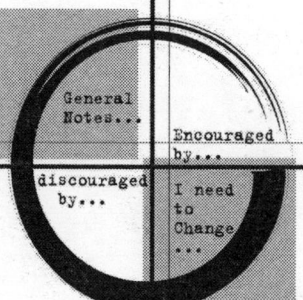

General Notes...

Encouraged by...

discouraged by...

I need to Change...

EVALUATE

✓ Get it RIGHT!

Bad language

The big issue

Chris had been at college for just under a year. He was the only Christian on his course but had never made a real point of telling anyone. One day at break he and a couple of his mates were hanging around indoors, near a radiator, trying to stay warm. The conversation had started in a fairly light manner and had got around to the usual focus of discussion – girls. In graphic detail each of his friends recalled their latest 'pull' and what that actually involved. Chris said nothing; instead he occupied himself with a Mars bar. Charlie, a highly strung and energetic guy, was busy swinging from a water pipe coming from the ceiling. Charlie, who had been watching Chris, suddenly asked the others, 'Have you noticed Chris never says much?' Dropping down from the pipe he turned to Chris, who had now stopped eating his Mars bar.

'What do you want me to say?' Chris asked defensively, spraying chocolate particles out of his mouth.

'I've noticed something about you Chris, you're different!'

Each of the guys now started on Chris. 'Yeah, you are a bit!' one of them confirmed.

Charlie continued, 'You never tell a rude joke, never talk about which girl you'd like to spend the night with, never curse and you never swear!'

'Where is this leading?' Chris wondered, feeling his skin burn and thinking he would make a brilliant torch in the dark.

'But Chris you're OK, you still know how to have a laugh and enjoy life and that's good enough for me!' declared Charlie.

Talking point

- Have you ever found yourself in a position like Chris?
- Do your friends swear and curse in front of you?
- Do you find yourself forced to join in or are you able to hold back?

- Do you think there is anything wrong with swearing, gossiping and telling dirty jokes?
- What would you have done if you were Chris – joined in to be one of the lads (or girls), remained silent or taken a stand?
- If you never swore, told or laughed at a sick joke, or gossiped about someone, what would it do to your friendship with those who do?
- Would you actually have anything in common with your friends if you held back?

Bible point

Gossip and backbiting

Matthew 12:36–37 LB *'You must give account on Judgement Day for every idle word you speak. Your words now reflect your fate then: either you will be justified by them or you will be condemned'*

James 3:9–10 *'With the tongue we praise our Lord and Father, and with it we curse men ... out of the same mouth come praise and cursing'*

Proverbs 16:28 *'The perverse stir up dissension and gossips separate close friends'*

Swearing

Ephesians 4:29 LB *'Don't use bad language. Say only what is good and helpful to those you are talking to, and what will give them a blessing'*

Colossians 3:8 *'But now you must rid yourselves of all such things as these: anger, rage, malice, slander and filthy language from your lips'*

Unsuitable jokes

Matthew 12:34 *'Out of the overflow of the heart the mouth speaks'*

Proverbs 9:12 *' ... if you are a mocker, you alone will suffer'*

Blasphemy

Deuteronomy 5:11 *'You shall not misuse the name of the Lord your God, for the Lord will not hold anyone guiltless who misuses his name'*

Negative actions

Phil 2:14 *'Do everything without complaining or arguing'*

Listening point

Unless you live your life in a monastery then swearing, rude jokes and general gossip will probably surround you every day. And let's face it, some words sound great and can describe just how you feel. 'Oh sugar!' just doesn't work when something hard and sharp drops on your foot amputating your toe. 'Goodness me!' doesn't describe the emotion going through your body when your best mate just stole your girlfriend or boyfriend and 'heck!' really isn't what you want to say when your dad finds out you skipped class and failed an exam. If you use any of those words around your mates then you may as well join a monastery because you can guarantee you are going to face serious abuse for having such a 'girlie' vocabulary.

When someone pulls you aside and tells you a really funny joke, which is either rude, sick or religious you just can't help laughing. It may be a little tasteless but nobody will ever know or care, right?

What about when you are told the juiciest piece of information about someone else? Is it wrong to keep it to yourself? Someone told you so you are obliged to tell someone else. The fact they said it was a 'secret' is code for meaning everyone should know as soon as possible.

Somewhere deep down within (and for some it is very deep) something tells us swearing, sick jokes and gossip are wrong. But because it is fairly deep it doesn't take much for us to ignore it especially because if we don't play our part among our friends we will be seen as weirdos and become outcasts.

'Is it really a big deal? I mean what's in a word or a comment?' Most of us don't even think twice when we hear obscene language at the cinema or on TV. We probably don't even think twice or even realise when we do it. But before we dismiss it as some kind of social historical nonsense, let's just examine that question, 'What's in a word?' Most swear words describe something offensive or disgusting either sexually or physically. For example, in just one sentence from an actor in a recent film words are used that refer to human excrement, sexual intercourse, eternal damnation and a fatherless child. None of these words form part of his message but are used as a sort of punctuation or breathing space. In this case it's meaningless and when you digest the translation it's offensive to listen to, so why say it? The Bible says we should rid ourselves of filthy language (Colossians 3:8). Not all bad language is used in a meaningless fashion though; we can use words to describe how we feel about someone, or what we would like to happen to someone. But to do that is to curse a person, and that's not something God would want us to do either. Again the Bible tells us to use our words as a blessing so as to 'build up' people (Ephesians 4:29). When God created humankind uniquely with the ability to speak, he didn't do it so we could use foul and offensive language, gossip and be destructive or sick in talking about people or events. Such actions only lead to other people's pain as well as ultimately our own. Wrong words have caused wars, murder, emotional and physical pain, abuse, divorce, and the break-up of friendships, to mention just a few.

There's a lot in a word or comment and we would only be fooling ourselves if we thought that what we say doesn't matter; it certainly matters to God. He cares greatly about what your every word does to others, but he also cares about what it does to you. Take a look at what the words we speak do to us:

They reveal our **Attitudes** – The Bible tells us what comes out of our mouth reflects our hearts.

They show what we **Value** – What we say tells others what we value.

They affect our **Godliness** – The Bible instructs us to 'Be Holy because I, the Lord your God, am Holy' (Leviticus 19:2). The word *holy* simply means to be 'set apart' or different from others, for God. It's difficult to be like that while we act like, or even worse than, others.

Sometimes you may be made fun of for being different. Not joining in on jokes and even putting a stop to gossip or backbiting will more than likely make you unpopular. The book of Proverbs says that doing so 'invites insults' (9:7). But there comes a time when we should take a stand for who we are and what we believe to be right. Do you remember Shadrach, Meshach and Abednego in the story of Daniel? They were three Jews in a hostile land who were told by the king to worship a golden statue or die. This is how they responded– 'O Nebuchadnezzar we do not need to defend ourselves before you in this matter. If we are thrown into the blazing furnace, the God we serve is able to save us from it, and he will rescue us from your hand, O king. But even if he does not, we want you to know, O king, that we will not serve your gods or worship the image of gold you have set up' (Daniel 3:16-18).

(For the whole story, see Daniel 2:48–3:30.)

Don't let others dictate your actions but choose how to act and what to say based on what you believe the Bible says to be true. Let your friends see just how important your faith is by the way you live your life.

One final thing you should know as a Christian is that it isn't just bad language, gossip or sick jokes that offend God. He is deeply wounded by how you use or speak his name. 'For God's sake!' or 'Jesus

Christ!' spoken in any other way than in respect is to blaspheme (offend or curse) his name. Imagine if every time someone was depressed, angry or hurt themselves they spouted out your name! Six billion people doing it every day would hardly give any kind of credit or worth to who you are. To put it bluntly, you and I are just humans, we have an abundance of failures and limits, but God has none. His name represents who he is and to misuse his name is to disrespect and disbelieve in who and what he is. Every wrong use of his name is to say he is something lower and less meaningful than he actually is. It is such a big deal to God that he included using his name correctly as part of the commandments (Deuteronomy 5:11). Next time you want to say 'God' or 'Christ' out of turn, bite your tongue. Don't do it and don't let others around you do it!

You need to be cool, and you certainly need to have fun, but God requires you to be radical in the way you speak. What you say determines who you are and what you are – can people see Christ living inside of you by your everyday words? If they can't, then something needs to change!

Radical Action Guide

Before you say anything ask yourself:
1. Will what I say hurt or upset anyone unnecessarily?
2. Would I be embarrassed if a certain person heard me?
3. If Jesus was visible would I be confident to go ahead and say it?
4. Is what I'm going to say positive?
5. Is it actually worth saying in the first place?

the Fiery tongue

HOW MANY TIMES DO YOU:-

Gossip and Backbite?	4 10 + Times a day	3 5 + Times a day
	2 1 + Times a day	1 0-6 Times a week

Swear?	4 10 + Times a day	3 5 + Times a day
	2 1 + Times a day	1 0-6 Times a week

Tell unsuitable Joke?	4 10 + Times a day	3 5 + Times a day
	2 1 + Times a day	1 0-6 Times a week

Have negative actions?	4 10 + Times a day	3 5 + Times a day
	2 1 + Times a day	1 0-6 Times a week

4 - Cool Tongue

5-7 Warm Tongue

8-10 Hot Tongue *Take a drink*

11-13 Boiling Tongue *ice cubes needed*

14-16 Tongue on Fire *call 999*

Add up all the numbers in the top hand corner that you feel fits your description **Total=**

Think it through...

- General Notes...
- Encouraged by...
- discouraged by...
- I need to Change...

EVALUATE

✓ Get it RIGHT!

Church

The big issue

Ever since he could remember, Andy had been forced to go to church. His mum and dad went, so that meant he had to go. The older Andy became, the more active his dad became in the church. He started out reading, then preaching and now he was an elder. His dad had told him the Bible says elders should be respectable mature leaders who have their lives in good order. That also means his children should have their lives in a good order. 'Pressure!' thought Andy. The truth of the matter was he hated church. He didn't hate God – far from it – every day he prayed and read his Bible and on Sundays he went to youth group. Yet church just seemed so boring and so removed from everyday reality. What could he do? Even though he was sixteen years old he felt that he had to attend the services out of respect for his father and his role in the church. And after all, however boring it was, it was only once a week.

Talking point

- ◆ Was Andy doing the right thing?
- ◆ Is your attitude to church in any way similar to Andy's?
- ◆ What do you think you would have done if you had been in Andy's shoes?
- ◆ In your opinion what should church be like?

Seriously Extreme

◆ What are some of the things that make church hard to stomach?

	Agree	Disagree
Church is boring		
Church services are too long		
Most of the time I don't understand what is happening		
The people never seem friendly		
The building is cold and unattractive		
The songs we sing are so old and high pitched they hurt your throat		
The minister isn't interested in young people and it shows in the service		
Nothing to do		
Add		

◆ What are some of the things you really enjoy about church?

Bible point

Matthew 16:18 *Jesus said, 'On this rock I will build my church'*
When he said the word 'church', he didn't mean a cold building with stained-glass windows and an out-of-tune organ. When he said 'church' he meant 'an assembly of people'. So Church means PEOPLE.

Acts 2:42 *'They devoted themselves to the apostles' teaching and to the fellowship, to the breaking of bread and to prayer'*
'They' means the first Christians.

Acts 2:44 *'All the believers were together and had everything in common'*
To the believers in Acts 'church' was an occasion where everyone came together, listened to teaching, had a great time, ate, prayed and remembered what Jesus had done for them. It was a lifestyle, not a weekly routine. Church was not a rigid formality but a 'place' where people could be real, laugh, cry, and worship God in a free and natural way. Wouldn't it be great if that was what church was like for everyone today?

1 Corinthians 12:27 *'Now you are the body of Christ, and each one of you is a part of it'*

The church is a big body and you are, as the Bible says, 'a part of it'. 1 Corinthians 12:1–31 tells us again and again that each member of the Church has a role to play. That means in your church God wants you not just to sit and receive but actually to be involved using the gifts that God has given you.

Listening point

So many young people would rather have a hole in their head than have to go to a church service. Even as a Christian the 'hole in the head' option can seem more attractive. Why do you have to go? You're supposed to go to worship God, but that can be fairly hard if you're bored out of your brains or so cold that your shivering is knocking the icicles off your nose.

Church is supposed to be a place where you grow spiritually, a place where you can worship God and feel able to pray alongside other people. Sometimes that doesn't happen for various reasons such as the ones already mentioned, the style isn't great or the building is too cold, but other times the blockage can be due to us. Church can be the most amazing place to be; the music's great, the speaker's excellent, people really like each other and it's warm, but most of all you sense that God is in the building. If that's what it is like for you then that's great, because church is supposed to be extremely positive where you are stretched, challenged, encouraged and drawn closer to God. But if it isn't like that and you're really not getting the best out of it, then take a check on yourself. If you're fast asleep on the back row with a few of your mates is it because things are so painful that the service knocked you clean out or because you were whacked from the late night before? Do you struggle with the sermon because the guy is rubbish or because he is considerably older than twenty? Does the music irritate you because it's a terrible tune with terrible lyrics you just don't understand or because it's not in the charts? Do the people in the congregation bother you because they are rude and snotty or because they have false teeth, wear glasses and the trendy clothes they wear were last in with the dinosaurs?!

It's actually quite easy to think about the negative things because often they are the things that slap us in the face like a wet fish. And I'm sure if you have a list like the one we've already looked at, or you have added to the list, each of your points are true and valid. Yet your church will also have many positive aspects to it. One of those aspects could be you.

Jesus said, 'It is better to give than to receive' (Acts 20:35). Why? Because in giving others receive, but also the opposite is true, in giving you receive! If you are struggling with your church, rather than thinking about not going any more why don't you consider more about what you can do and how you can help? You've probably heard it said a thousand times before that 'young people are the Church of tomorrow!' Although that may be true, it's also true that 'you are the church of today'. Your happiness is vital for if you leave today, there may well not be a church tomorrow. Use your gifts and get involved; help to build and develop the church rather than leave or pull it down. It's important, though, to remember the church is a family and like all families you don't always agree with each other. But rather than throw a fist and pull a wig, show patience and a little bit of love. Be an active part of your church, un-block any blockages you may be causing and soon enough church will be a place where you grow rather than sleep!

Radical Action Guide

1. If you don't like church work out what it is you really don't like.
2. Is that reason a good one? If you think it is and things should change then come up with a positive proposal.
3. If it isn't a good reason and you realise you need to change, then find someone to talk to about how you feel and discuss together ways you could start viewing things more positively.
4. Hold off on the criticism and get down from the spectators' gallery; find ways in which you can get more involved in the life of the church.
5. Remember you are a vitally important person and your opinion counts. So don't be embarrassed to disagree but be humble as well as confident.
6. Being with other believers can be difficult at times but it's what God asks of us, so take time to listen to other people to see how they view things.
7. If you have given it your best shot and things really don't work out and you are still not happy, then as a last option, after talking with the minister or youth leader, think about finding another church which would suit you, and where you personally could worship God in a more enjoyable and relaxed environment. Leaving a church is never nice but ultimately it's far more important that you grow in your faith.

In what way could you become more involved in your Church?

Tick next to the activities you are currently or would like to be involved with

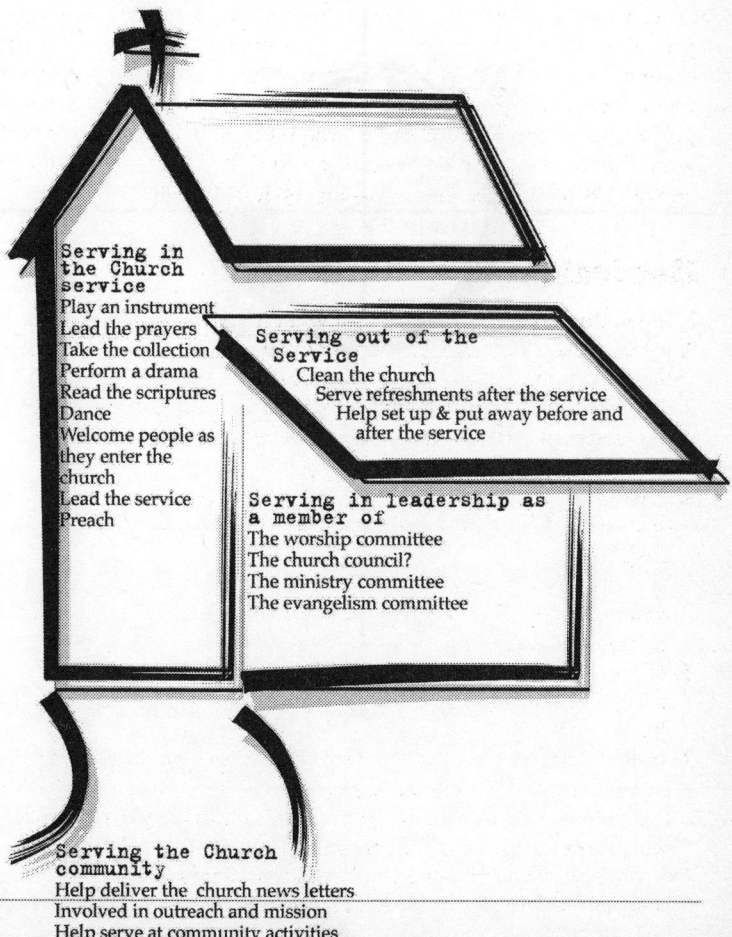

Serving in the Church service
Play an instrument
Lead the prayers
Take the collection
Perform a drama
Read the scriptures
Dance
Welcome people as they enter the church
Lead the service
Preach

Serving out of the Service
Clean the church
Serve refreshments after the service
Help set up & put away before and after the service

Serving in leadership as a member of
The worship committee
The church council?
The ministry committee
The evangelism committee

Serving the Church community
Help deliver the church news letters
Involved in outreach and mission
Help serve at community activities
(OAP meals/job club/mums & tots
Church

Think it through...

	General Notes...	Encouraged by...
	discouraged by...	I need to Change...

EVALUATE

Get it RIGHT!

Drink, Drugs and Cigarettes

The big issue

After the youth group on Sunday night James was heading home. As he was leaving, he said his goodbyes to his friends and the youth workers. A couple of new guys, Todd and Matt, came alongside him and asked if he wanted to go on to a party. James didn't know them very well and had come to the conclusion from the way they acted that they were probably not Christians. On that basis he wanted to be a good example and show them that Christians could have a laugh as much as anyone else. He agreed to go.

The party was less than a mile away in the house of another bloke whom Todd and Matt knew – it was a small house and James was surprised that not many people were actually there. As he walked into the living room Todd thrust a bottle of beer into his hand and offered him a cigarette. James declined the cigarette but accepted the beer on the grounds that it couldn't do him any harm and what kind of example would he be as a Christian if he asked for lemonade? The more James drank the more relaxed he became. Everyone else was smoking and as he relaxed James felt the pressure to have a cigarette; it would just prove how cool he really was. He had never smoked before and his first lungful was far from pleasant, in fact it made him feel instantly sick. Todd and Matt just laughed as he coughed on the smoke.

'Cigarettes are for babies,' Matt said, taking the light from him.

'This is for men,' Todd said, showing James a plastic bag. James's eyesight was already blurred and he was struggling to concentrate. 'What is it?' he asked, slurring his words. 'Cannabis, you idiot!' Matt joked. 'Are you going to try it or are you too much of a Jesus wimp?'

Though by now James's reactions were slow, Matt's challenge grated on him. 'Jesus wimp, what does he mean Jesus wimp? What am I doing here half drunk? He's not interested in Jesus or my example!'

The penny dropped, and James realised what a fool he had been. He made for the door; he really did feel quite dizzy now. As he left, he could hear them both jeering at him and mocking his faith. James stumbled home drunk, embarrassed and ashamed.

Talking point

- Do you think that James's attempt at being cool was a good thing or not?
- Was James too hard on himself thinking that he had been a 'fool'?
- Which of the following do you think are OK for Christians to do and why?

	Yes	No	Why
Drink alcohol			
Smoke cigarettes			
Take illegal drugs for pleasure			

- Have you ever had experience with any of these?
- Are any of these bad for your health? Should that be a reason not to take them?
- What does each of them (alcohol, cigarettes and drugs) actually do to you? Is that good or bad?

Bible point

Alcohol
'Do not get drunk on wine, which leads to debauchery. Instead, be filled with the Spirit' Ephesians 5:18.
'Who has woe? Who has sorrow? Who has strife? Who has complaints? Who has needless bruises? Who has bloodshot eyes? Those who linger over wine, who go to sample bowls of mixed wine ... In the end it bites like a snake and poisons like a viper. Your eyes will see strange sights and your mind imagine confusing things. You will be like one sleeping on the high seas, lying on top of the rigging ... When will I wake up so I can find another drink?' Proverbs 23:29-35.

Cigarettes
'Do you not know that your body is a temple of the Holy Spirit, who is in you, whom you have received from God?' 1 Corinthians 6:19.
'No temptation has seized you except what is common to man. And God is faithful; he will not let you be tempted beyond what you can bear. But when you are tempted, he will also provide a way out so that you can stand up under it' 1 Corinthians 10:13.

Drugs
'I have come that they may have life, and have it to the full' John 10:10.
'Be self-controlled and alert' 1 Peter 5:8.
Everyone must be subject to to the governing authorities, for there is no authority except that which God has established... Consequently whoever who rebels against the authority is rebelling against what God has instituted ... Do you want to be free from fear of the one in authority? Then do what is right and you will be commended.' Romans 13:1-3.

Seriously Extreme

Listening point

A sad and simple fact of reality is that drinking, smoking and taking drugs are as much a part of people's lives as the clothes they wear. Who hasn't been offered drugs in school? Or at least had one puff on a cigarette with a few mates? And everybody's got drunk at some time or other – right? Most people have, that's for sure, and that includes Christians as well as people who wouldn't claim to be Christians. Most of us have had some involvement with at least one of the above, such as drinking a little bit too much and having the contents of your last meal all over your clothes. The Bible has a strong view that certainly isn't popular. But if you claim to be a believer who loves Jesus, then you had better get up to speed with how God feels about it.

Ultimately each of us know the score; we don't need to read the Bible to find out. We have a conscience that niggles us when we are buying a pint under age, or drinking way too much. And when you 'nearly die' when you bump into your minister with a cig dangling out of your mouth – that says something doesn't it? Not everyone is into drugs, but if you've ever taken them, I bet you didn't announce it in youth group or Bible study! 'Don't rock the status quo' may seem to be the motto, but the truth is that you know deep down it's wrong. Why?

'Do not get drunk on wine, which leads to debauchery' (Ephesians 5:18). In other words, if you get plastered, you do things out of your control, and if you are out of control then you may do just about any kind of wrong thing. It ain't all doom and gloom though, in small doses alcohol is actually fine for people, but go over the line and you can be flat on your back or with your head down the toilet the next day. But remember, you don't even need to be terribly drunk for your balance, vision and decision-making abilities to be thrown to the wind. Excessive drinking certainly damages your body, especially your liver, and can easily become addictive. Christians around the world disagree about whether drinking a small amount is *wrong*, full stop, that's for you to decide. But before you down a pint in the pub, remember, under-age drinking is still illegal.

You may think that smoking makes you look cool, but your body certainly won't agree. Anyway, remember God – unlike everybody else – isn't interested in how you look. He's far more concerned about the state of your soul (1 Samuel 16:7). The expression, 'I'm dying for a fag' couldn't be nearer to the truth. Every time you inhale the smoke you pollute your body with toxic gases that weaken your heart, dramatically increase the chances of lung cancer, and radically reduce your chances of living as long as Mr or Mrs Average. Think about other people: not everyone likes breathing a smoker's smoke! Ultimately remember your body is the temple of the Holy Spirit (1 Corinthians 6:19), look after it, don't destroy it!

Drug taking could take you on a great rollercoaster 'trip' leaving you feeling absolutely great. Whether solvent, soft or hard, taken orally or injected, if thrill is what you want then it's a thrill you're likely to get. Until you run into trouble. Drugs are not safe and as well as polluting the body they can cause extensive brain and tissue damage, addiction, and in some cases death. But God offers an alternative which is neither illegal nor harmful. Experience it for yourself (John 10:10).

Whether what you want is a drink, a fag or some weird and wonderful drug that sends you into cuckoo-land for a while, take a moment to ask yourself just why you want it. God didn't intend fun to involve you in damaging your own body, breaking the law or for it to be artificial and over after several hours. He has his own ideas on fun. That is, he gives us himself and all that comes with him. Sounds a bit twee, eh? Well it does, and to the observer it is, but it isn't twee for those who look for him and his life to the max! Sure, we might not feel like surfing clouds as soon as we wake up or flying through space throughout the day every day. What Jesus offers can't be compared to drugs or alcohol, it's a whole different experience. It isn't a thrill or a once-in-a-lifetime event. The closer we draw to him the more he hugs us with his love which seems to reach deep down into the cracks of our lives. What kind of cracks? Cracks of insecurity, emptiness, dejection and rejection, lack of meaning and direction, no hope or real belief in self. Have you ever felt any of those things? You're human, so of course you have. These cracks are painful, they hurt, we do our best to cover them up but they usually ooze out blood and pus, and never seem to go away. When he finds those parts in our lives, his touch is unexplainable as it begins to replace the scabs and wounds with the exact opposites such as a deep kind of happiness, a sense of meaning and purpose, a bright belief in the future, self and others, as well as a peace that cannot be described on the pages of this book. When you have that, and it's there for the taking, the highs of getting drunk or taking a 'trip' are completely shallow but more importantly the reasons why you might want to do those things are no longer so attractive or real or relevant! Jesus' idea of life to the full includes dealing head-on with the reasons behind the fact that people so often end up puking their guts out after a night out with the lads.

The Bible has a story of a young man called Daniel who had been specially selected because he was good looking, bright and fit. He was to be an educated nobleman in the king's palace but one of the rules was that he must eat the food and wine from the king's table. Daniel did not wish to pollute his body with the type of food he was given. He made his stand insisting on nothing other than water and vegetables. At the end of a ten day trial Daniel looked healthier and fitter than all those who enjoyed the king's feasts (see Daniel 1:3-17).

Daniel was a young man of God who went against the pleasures that everyone else enjoyed and was far better for it. As Christians, it can be so tempting to be like James, in not wanting to appear a church-going jerk. But actually by joining in, James became much more of a jerk. The Bible says, 'In everything set them an example by doing what is good' (Titus 2:7).

But this is easier said than done; reality, as James found, is very different. The 'just say no' motto isn't so easy when you are with a group of mates who have a different idea about getting a kick out of life than you do as a Christian. Here are a few ideas for being a little bit firmer and more sure in the 'No!' reply.

Radical Action Guide

1. Make sure you pray daily and ask God for your strength.
2. Make sure you belong to a good youth fellowship group so you are continually growing in your faith sharing with other teenagers facing the same problems and praying for each other.
3. Make sure you have Christian friends with whom you can make a 'No' pact and who can both encourage and check up on you.
4. Make sure you know for yourself what it means to have a faith worth saying 'No' for.
5. Make sure you have an answer prepared that doesn't make you 'Mr Corny of the Year' but still keeps you firm when the offer is made and the pressure is on.
6. Make sure you don't make things harder for yourself by walking into situations you know will be difficult.
7. Make sure your closest mates are Christians who believe what you believe and aren't continually out to change you.

At the end of the day the thing – whatever it is – that people are asking you to do may be wrong, it may be illegal, it may be bad for you but all the same it's tough to say no when everyone else is doing it. Don't use any of these three as your key reasons for saying no to drugs, excessive and underage drinking or smoking. Use the fact that you love Jesus and want to please him more than your mates or even yourself. You may feel a real idiot, you may not get struck with a divine bolt of heavenly ecstasy. You may even feel a total isolated jerk for turning the invitation down as your friends laugh or exclude you. But you did it! You stood your ground, and you can be sure God saw everything that happened. Remember the Bible says we won't be tempted beyond what we can cope with (1 Corinthians 10:13); you may feel as if you're getting pretty close to your limit but when you do, Jesus is right there beside you. And when you turn to him rather than give into the crowd, he will faithfully take you to a whole new depth of life. How you feel about yourself and others will change; it could be a quick change or it could be gradual. But rest assured booze and drugs aren't ever going to do that, and if they do, it will be a change for the worse. Regardless of what our friends do we should stand our ground and take the full life that he gives – there is nothing to match it! Make that decision to be different from the rest.

Relying on the Fullness of God

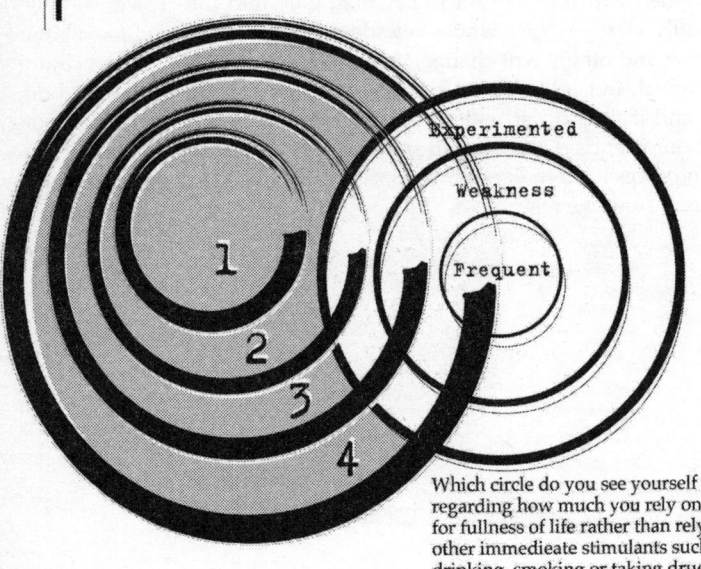

Which circle do you see yourself in regarding how much you rely on God for fullness of life rather than relying on other immedieate stimulants such as drinking, smoking or taking drugs?

1. Relying on the fullness of God
2. Mostly rely on God's fullness *but have experimented with stimulants*
3. Sometimes rely on God's fullness *but have a weakness to stimulants*
4. Never rely on God's fullness *and frequently take stimulants*

What are the cracks in your life that you need Jesus to deal with?

If you are not relying entirely on God but looking towards alternative feel-good stimulants, what needs to change?

Think it through...

General Notes...	Encouraged by...
discouraged by...	I need to Change...

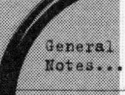

EVALUATE

✓ Get it RIGHT!

Encouragement

The big issue

Louise was dreading school. She knew the results from her maths exam were due. She also knew she had done very badly. Louise was bright and intelligent but nobody had ever helped her realise just how bright she was. Every time she didn't understand something she was too scared to ask for an explanation for fear of looking even more stupid than she thought she already was. Louise was also a loner with no real friends to hang around with at break and no one liked to sit with her in class. She hated school, hated herself and hated life.

The maths lesson was the last of the day. The teacher started by reading out the results – everyone was getting high marks – the lowest pupil so far had received 76 per cent, and then it came to Louise. The teacher made a dramatic announcement, 'Louise, you have the most outstanding result beating everyone else by far'. He paused and everyone in the class waited to hear how well she had done, 'Yes you have beaten everyone for the last place with an unbelievable total of 33 per cent. Well done, I'm sure your parents will be proud. Don't work so hard next time!' His sarcasm cut like a knife, wounding Louise deeply, while the rest of the class burst into laughter. After class as Louise began to leave the room, another girl, Danni, who was bright, good-looking and popular, came alongside and asked if she was OK. Louise had never been asked anything other than for a rubber or pencil in six months by any other student in her class. She was immediately defensive wondering what prank she was going to be the butt of. 'I'm sorry about what just happened, you didn't deserve that!' Danni said.

A little taken aback, Louise just stared awkwardly, not knowing what to say. Danni, sensing Louise's embarrassment, cut in, 'Come on, let's walk to the bus station'. Most people wouldn't have thought twice about the invitation, but Louise hadn't ever walked home from school with anyone before, until now.

Talking point

- How would you have felt if you had been in Louise's shoes?

- What would it have taken for Louise to have been more happy in life?

- Do you know people like Louise in your school, youth group or social life? What could you do to help them?

- People need encouragement – just one encouraging word could change a person's entire day, week or even life. How often do you encourage people? Do you find it easy? How do you do it?

- Do you just encourage your friends? How could you encourage the people you don't like or who are a little 'weird' or 'odd'?

Bible point

James 3:9–10 – *'With the tongue we praise our Lord and Father, and with it we curse people, who have been made in God's likeness. Out of the same mouth come praise and cursing. My brother and sisters, this should not be'*

Have you ever started to dream while in the middle of your prayer time about someone who did something wrong to you and started to imagine all the strong words you would like to say to them? Or have you whispered to a friend in church about how awful someone in your class is? Maybe not, but after you've prayed or been to church, do you spend the whole day or week being nice, not saying a wrong word about anyone? If you don't then – I'm sorry to say – you're living with double standards! It's exactly what James says we can be like; one minute we praise God, the next minute we curse someone. Do you generally encourage people or pull them down?

1 Thessalonians 5:11 – *'Therefore encourage one another and build each other up'*

It's almost impossible, isn't it, to actually say something nice to someone? I mean, what would they think – weirdo, stranger, girlie, freak or something embarrassing like that? Not to mention what they might do! Relax, it doesn't mean we should tell everyone we love the way they have done their hair today or we like the way they tie their shoelaces. But it does mean if someone does something well, then tell them. If someone is struggling, or down in the dumps, then think of one thing you would want to hear if you were in their shoes at that moment and then go ahead and say it to them. You may find it hard to do but you have no idea the power your every word may have. ...

2 Timothy 1:3 – *'I thank God, whom I serve, as my ancestors did, with a clear conscience, as night and day I constantly remember you in my prayers'*
Imagine that someone really famous whom you admire and respect wrote you a letter that said every day they thought about you and thanked God for you in their prayers! That would be pretty amazing. That's how Paul (who was a big deal two thousand years ago) started a letter to his friend Timothy. Has anyone ever told you something so shocking that you didn't know what to say, because nothing you could say or do would help? But we can help, we can pray for them daily just like Paul did for Timothy. Is there anyone you could encourage today by telling them you will pray for them until their problem is solved?

Listening point

'A word aptly spoken is like apples of gold in settings of silver' (Proverbs 25:11). What on earth does that mean? Most of us have never seen golden apples so may struggle to imagine them in settings of silver. However, I think we can get the gist of what it's hinting at. Something so infinitely precious and important that to have it would have others turning green with envy. That's what it means for us to say the right words at the right time. It's a priceless gift and something we should all try to have. Louise's maths teacher certainly didn't have that gift, neither did the pupils in Louise's class. Louise had no self-esteem and because of this she had no motivation to do well at school or create good friendships. She felt like rubbish and believed she was rubbish. But just imagine if someone had encouraged her and said really nice and meaningful things to her – what a difference that would have made. Danni was the first person to give her the time of day and because of it became the first person to make her feel she wasn't quite the worthless ball of scum that everyone else made her believe she was, even if nobody had ever said it directly.

As Christians, we want to be people who make a difference and impact the world we live in for good. Yet it's far easier and much more natural for us to act as if we are not followers of Jesus by being negative, spiteful, and unapproachable to others. But then we are not being the kind of person Jesus wants us to be. He said we should shine out like the lights of a city on a hill but often we show as much light as a lamp which has been placed under a bowl (Matthew 5:14–15). Jesus said, 'Let your light shine before men, that they may see your good deeds and praise your Father in heaven' (Matthew 5:16). What would be a good deed to somebody? How about kindness, generosity, time and encouragement?

Just one simple appropriate and encouraging word to one person could also affect dozens of other people. How many grumpy people do you think you come across first thing in the morning? Too many! Rather than being rude or ignoring them give them a 'golden apple' and you just might change their grump and they may well in turn change someone else's grump and on the cycle could go. Always take time to look for the good in people and find a way of saying something positive. Anyone can be negative but only someone who really cares about life, people and ultimately God will be continually positive. Find the Louise in your world and change her life by the carefully chosen loving words you use. If you really want to be different and sold out for God, then this is the best starting point you're going to get. It's simple, it's radical, and it won't just change other people's lives, it will change yours as well.

Think about it for one moment. The person who inspires you the most, the person who has brought out the best in you is most probably the person who knows just how to encourage you, say the right thing at the right time, and make you feel fairly good about who you are. On almost every page of the gospels we see Jesus doing just that, looking into someone's life and saying the exact thing they needed to hear. It's actually quite easy – all it takes is for us to stop focusing on our own lives and tune into the lives of our friends and others around us. Remember, everyone needs to be loved and everyone needs encouragement. Nobody needs someone to be negative about them. It's not just people words can snub – ignoring or avoiding a person is a form of *neglect* and that is incredibly negative, and it definitely hurts. Be different from others, and if you're not different already, start now by being positive and encouraging towards the people in your world, whether they are your friends or the person no-one gives the time of day to.

Radical Action Guide

1. Be warm and kind to people.
2. Be quick to tell someone when they did well.
3. Be understanding and reassuring when someone did not do so well.
4. Be sensitive when someone is low and think about how you would feel if you were in their shoes and what you would need to hear in order to feel much better.
5. Offer to pray for people who have no solutions to their problems.
6. Ask God each day to give you the opportunity to encourage someone.
7. Be willing to accept encouragement when someone else gives it!

the encouragment spider

Choose 1 statement from each side to assess how you relate to people

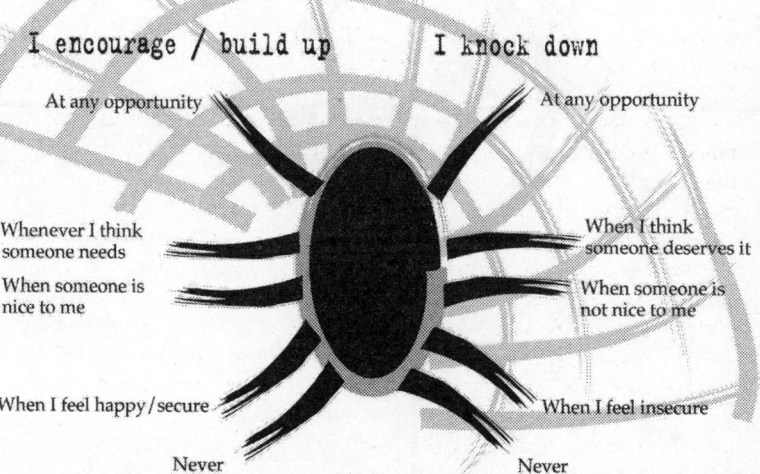

I encourage / build up — At any opportunity
Whenever I think someone needs
When someone is nice to me
When I feel happy/secure
Never

I knock down — At any opportunity
When I think someone deserves it
When someone is not nice to me
When I feel insecure
Never

How well do I receive encouragment from others?

Does my answer reflect my response to the illustration above?
In other words is my ability to encourage others similar to how I receive encouragement?

Am I content in how I seek to bring the best out in others?

Think it through...

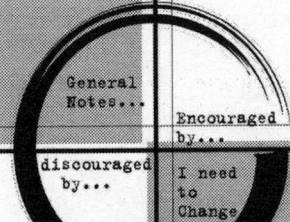

- General Notes...
- Encouraged by...
- discouraged by...
- I need to Change...

EVALUATE

✓ Get it RIGHT!

Forgiveness

The big issue

Michelle had been going out with Rob for several months now, people saw them as a steady couple. For that matter so did Michelle. They saw each other two or three nights through the week and spent the weekends together.

However, Rob announced one night over the phone he couldn't do anything this coming weekend as his family were heading south to visit his Gran. When the weekend came Michelle was left feeling a little bored and unsure of what to do with herself. Before she met Rob she used to spend every Saturday night with Emily, her best mate. As she thought about it she realized she had not paid much attention to Emily since starting to see her new boyfriend. Emily lived only five minutes walk away and Michelle decided to go and see her. She knocked at the door and waited, but there was no answer. But the lights were on and in the past she had been told to walk in if no one answered, so she did just that. 'Hello!' she called out.

There was no response. 'It's Michelle, Emily are you in?' Still no response, but as she went further into the house she could hear music upstairs. Realizing Emily was in and as usual had the music on too loud in her bedroom, Michelle went upstairs and opened the door.

'Hi, Emily it's Mich ...' Michelle froze, she did a double take as she could not believe what she saw. Emily was lying on the bed, kissing a bloke. But it wasn't just any bloke – it happened to be Rob, Michelle's boyfriend.

Talking point

- How do you think Michelle would have felt?
- How would you have responded?

- How should she respond in future to both Rob and Emily individually and as a new couple?
- Should she forgive them, and if so what does it mean to forgive? Does it mean she should still be their friend?
- What are the unforgivable things in this world?

Bible point

God forgives us
: *'If we confess our sins, he is faithful and just and will forgive our sins and purify us from all unrighteousness'* 1 John 1:9.
'Therefore there is now no condemnation for those who are in Christ Jesus' Romans 8:1.

We should forgive others
: *'A new command I give you: Love one another. As I have loved you, so you must love one another'* John 13:34.
'If you do not forgive others for their sins, your Father will not forgive your sins' Matthew 6:15.

Look what happens when we forgive
: *'If you forgive the sins of anyone their sins are forgiven (=released)'* John 20:23.

Listening point

'Get stuffed, I don't want to see you again.' Ever said that?

'You know what? I'm going to tell everyone what happened to you last summer!'

Ever felt like snitching? Of course you have, because when some jerk you don't like, or even worse a mate you do like, does something to really hurt you then all you want to do is to hit right back. Let's face it, you never asked them to do whatever they did, so when you find your best mate snogging with your girl or boyfriend, punching them on the nose seems a pretty fair response.

What other people say or do can cause a whole load of bad things to go on in our lives such as crying ourselves to sleep at night, or making us feel very small and unimportant. You feel fine one day, a loser the next, or a total wreck the day after.

'Forgiveness?' Forget it! It's neither natural nor practical, it goes against the grain and is about as attractive as a dog eating his own vomit! It was the apostle Peter who thought up that example (2 Peter 2:22). It's pretty strong stuff, but if we are really honest, when we have been hurt by someone forgiving them isn't the first thing that comes to mind. Eating the dog's vomit may seem easier than pardoning someone who has hurt me deeply. Yet it's number one on God's list of essential actions after someone has hurt us! Forgiveness is at the very centre of the Christian faith, without it our belief is not real. That may be true, but it doesn't help when you're suffering because someone has smashed your world apart. So let's take a closer look at six very simple and basic reasons that may help us to understand why God commands us to forgive -

1. Forgive because Jesus has forgiven us – At times it can be difficult to think that God has forgiven us for what we have done. The Bible tells us there is nothing we can do that God cannot forgive and nothing that will stop him loving us. So we should do the same.
2. Forgive because it is actually healthy for us – Refusing to forgive keeps feelings of anger and resentment churning and twisting deep within. Slowly they make us more bitter and can ultimately cause us to become physically ill.
3. Forgive because we want others to forgive us – Believe it or not, there may be people out there who feel hurt by your actions. Do you want them to hate you for it? 'Do to others what you would have them do to you' (Matthew 7:12). Forgive them and hope others will forgive you.
4. Forgive because if we don't it can lead us to do wrong – In his letter to the Christians in Galatia Paul instructs us to have qualities of the Holy Spirit such as 'love, joy, peace, patience, kindness, goodness, faithfulness gentleness and self control' (Galatians 5:22). Anger, resentment and hatred are feelings that are opposite to what God wants and can harm us.
5. Forgive because Jesus loves the person who has hurt us – 2 Corinthians 5:20 says we represent Jesus. If people know you are a Christian then they will judge you by your actions. How did you react towards that person? Did you get angry, curse or swear? How do you act towards them now? What image of Jesus are you showing them?
6. Forgive because unforgiveness restricts our spiritual growth – If we are filled with bad feelings about others, drawing close to God becomes so much more difficult. Jesus told us 'to love your enemies and pray' for them (Matthew 5:44). If we aren't forgiving we aren't loving and therefore we aren't trying to do what Jesus asked us to.

Sadly our growth slows right down until we face the issue head on and forgive the person who hurt us.

Forgiveness is a choice. You don't have to do it. You can say you've done it and not mean it. Even if you do mean it the pain may not leave. But when you forgive something happens deep down within and your attitude to the other person begins to change.

Once you have chosen to forgive someone ask God to help you do it. Tell him you want to forgive them and then give the incident to him. He will take the situation out of your hands, and from then on every time you feel angry or resentful remember he now holds the 'rights' to the situation, not you, because you gave it to him. So kill the mental video replay which stirs all your feelings again, by remembering that you forgave, and that is that!

Nobody said forgiveness is easy, but you will be a far better person for it. The person you forgave may never even know they hurt you or, even worse, they may never care. However, God saw your actions and is proud of you for what you did! Make a stand, give up the hurt and anger and forgive, regardless of the outcome!

Radical Action Guide

1. Ask God to show you someone who has hurt you whom you haven't forgiven, or ask him to show you someone you just don't like and what it is you don't like about them.
2. Ask God to help you forgive them.
3. Tell God in so many words that you forgive them.
4. Ask God to help you forget the incident.
5. If you can't, then find a wise friend and share the problem. Together pray through the situation.
6. If you're still struggling to forgive, then go and find the person who hurt you. Don't blame them but try to resolve the problem and be willing to say sorry for anything you have done wrong.

Reaction page

Can I can't I? GRAPH

Many people hold a grading system in their lives for what is forgivable, what can be forgiven over time and what can never be forgiven under any circumstance. Take a look at the graph below and fill in each area with an issue you could or couldn't forgive, by writing a word below the category. For example:

Easily forgiven = a friend forgetting to phone
Never forgive = Being used and dumped

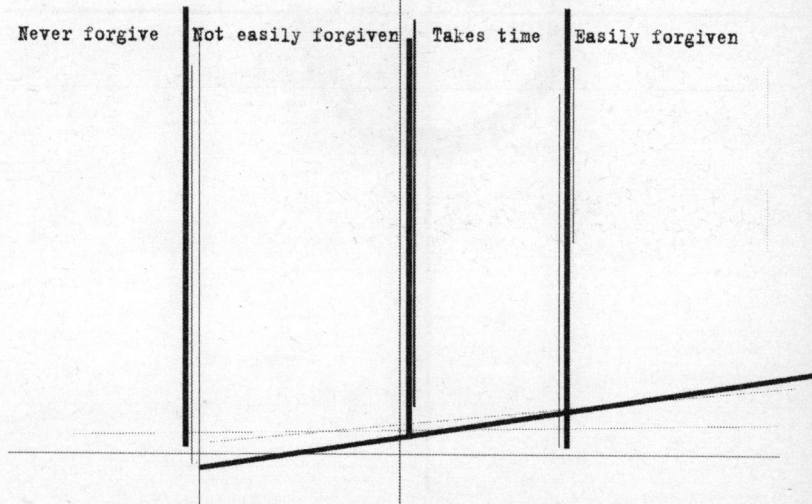

Never forgive	Not easily forgiven	Takes time	Easily forgiven

If Jesus turned up right now and examined your heart would you be in any way embarrassed or ashamed because of the unforgivingness and resentment you have about other people?

Now look again and ask the question, 'What help would I need or what would it take for me to actually be able to forgive what I have written in my *Never Forgiven* area? Be honest!

If you have not written anything in the *Never Forgiven* section but yet you have things in your life that you haven't forgiven, then what help do you need to start the process of forgiving?

Think it through...

General Notes...	Encouraged by...
discouraged by...	I need to Change...

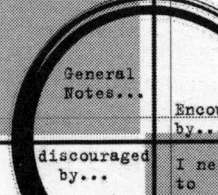

EVALUATE

✓ Get it RIGHT!

Guilt

The big issue

Paul had been new at the youth group and had been directly to blame for three meetings ending in chaos. He was disruptive to say the least. Little he said was either intelligent or positive. He swore, cursed everyone and everything, and threw objects around with no care for their value. The youth leaders became terrified of his turning up. Anything they had prepared was sure to end in failure. Paul had a natural gift for disruption.

Eventually one of the leaders took Paul aside and told him if he caused any more trouble they would have to speak to his parents. Paul's displays of emotion had been nothing compared to what the leader was now confronted with. Like a firework gone wrong Paul spewed insult on insult upon the leaders and the church. 'Hold on a minute,' the leader urged. 'It's OK, whatever it is, it's OK!' Paul cooled off for a moment and then broke down in tears.

And so Paul and the youth leader began to talk. Bit by bit Paul poured out his heart. From the age of three he could remember his father shouting and screaming at his mother about how expensive having children was and how demanding they were.

'Get rid of them! Get rid of them!' he would say. By the time Paul was five, his father left home shouting that he no longer wanted to feed 'the little brats'. His mother tried to raise three children on her own, without any support. When Paul was ten his mum had become so exhausted and beaten by life that she was admitted into a psychiatric hospital. Paul and his two brothers were placed into care. His mother was still in hospital and he was still in care.

The leaders met with Paul over the course of three months and he slowly began to change. For ten years he had lived with the belief that it was his fault his father had left and his mother had become ill. The greatest day of Paul's life came when he finally realised that perhaps he wasn't to blame after all.

Talking point

- What feelings do you think Paul must have experienced from the time his father left till the day he exploded at the leader?
- Have you ever felt like Paul in any way?
- Has there been a time in your life when you have really let someone down? How did you feel, and why?
- Are guilt and embarrassment things that should stay with us throughout life?
- How can we best deal with our guilt and shame?

Bible point

Romans 3:23 – *'For all have sinned and fall short of the glory of God'*
It's important to realize that failing, making mistakes and doing things wrong is as much a part of our world as the air we breathe. Nobody's perfect – we'd all like to be but we are not!

Jeremiah 31:34 – *'I will forgive their wickedness and will remember their sins no more'*
If you are a Christian, then the Bible says again and again that by God's grace (his overwhelming and unlimited kindness) all of your sins are forgiven and what's more he forgets whatever you did wrong. He simply cannot remember what you did!

Hebrews 10:22 – *'Let us draw near to God with a sincere heart in full assurance of faith, having our hearts sprinkled to cleanse us from a guilty conscience'*
With God, forgiveness means to forget as if it never happened. In other words, once we have been forgiven we have no reason at all to feel guilty.

Psalm 103:12 – *'As far as the east is from the west, so far has He removed our transgressions from us'*
When God forgives he really does forgive, it's as distant as we can possibly imagine. If he forgives, forgets and throws your sin as far away as it can go, then what logical point does guilt and embarrassment serve in our lives?

Listening point

'I feel so guilty!' We have all been there, each with our own reasons.

Laughing at the school geek, double crossing a mate, back-biting about someone who hears every word, having a cheap joke at a friend's expense when he doesn't do so well at something that you find easy, scratching the paintwork on your dad's car or forgetting to pass on a really important message, and when you do remember it, it's just too late.

Oops! You shrug your shoulders, what do you care?

But the fact is you do care, and the more you shrug the more it bothers you. Yes that's guilt all right, it bothers you so much it just won't go away – it sticks like dog dirt to your shoe! That's an unpleasant thought, but guilt's an even nastier feeling.

Everyone has a conscience and most people don't deliberately want to hurt another person, but we do, and when we do our conscience lets us know what we did was wrong. The problem for most of us is that we never find a way either to forget or to get rid of the bad feeling inside. Without warning, what we did can pop right back into our minds, with exactly the same feelings of guilt and regret we had at the time. Guilt has the unfortunate ability to twist and turn within us. It can give you emotions you never thought you had, such as a deep anger within yourself. Like a nuclear reactor, melt-down is never far away! It can reduce the happy character that was once you into a depressive grey lump. 'You blew it' you continually tell yourself like a tea addict plunging the same bag into the pot for the twentieth time that day. You have re-lived that experience to the point of despair, you feel terrible and have no sense of worth at all. You end up thinking, feeling and deserving to be labelled as 'rubbish'! 'How could you do it?' What a question, and what a feeling – you're resentful, you're bitter but ultimately you are hurting!

It's like a poison slowly but surely killing the good and kind person within us. It's very important that we find and take the antidote to stop the crippling of our character. 'But they just don't know what I have done!' you may be thinking. 'Everyone hates me and I hate myself.' Well, no matter what you have done, not everyone hates you. God loves you unconditionally – in fact the Bible tells us that nothing can stop God loving you (Romans 8:38–39). 'Ah, just words ... words I have heard a thousand times!' you may think. Yes, and if you have sinned a thousand times and more, it's for you that Jesus died on the cross. By dying Jesus showed his love, because each time you failed, each time you got it wrong, for that moment and for that incident he hung in agony until he died, and in his death he brought complete forgiveness. No guilt, no condemnation, just pure freedom from the sin that traps us. Another way of looking at it, one death but a million wrongs covered!

That's wonderful, but there's another problem. What if it isn't just God I offended and hurt, but somebody else? What if that person could never forgive me and I could never forgive myself?' The reality is that we do hurt people and occasionally the pain we have caused may damage them to the point of being unable to forgive. All you can do is to try to correct the wrong you have caused and confess your regret and sorrow. For some that will never be enough but for God it is always enough. If you have done all you can and asked God to forgive you for the wrong you caused another person (because it's still sin) then he will forgive you and he will offer to take away the guilt that lives within you, even if the other person or people still hate or blame you.

Lots of people for all sorts of different reasons feel like Paul did – guilty for things that have happened to them which were beyond their control. It may be about a divorce, the sickness or death of someone they loved, or a car crash in which they were simply a passenger. Whatever the situation, for whatever reason, they have come to believe it was their fault. If that's how you feel, it may take more than this book to help you, but it never was or will be your fault that it happened. Paul wasn't a part of the decision his mother and father took when deciding to have a family. He wasn't a part of the reason his father struggled with the issues of raising and supporting his children, nor was he the reason his mother was broken and beaten by life. Paul was a casualty, but yet felt guilty. The same is certainly going to be true of you. Speak with someone and let them help you get to the issue that fills you with guilt every time you remember that painful moment.

No good can ever come from a life of guilt. It slowly but surely beats us and changes us into something cold and ugly inside, but Jesus offers us an alternative – a chance to be a new person inside, without any condemnation, guilt or negative feelings. With him, no matter what you have done there is always forgiveness and a chance to remove the wrong from your life for ever! So why not start now and see the difference Jesus can make to your guilt?

Radical Action Guide

1. Write down anything you feel guilty about.
2. Whom have you hurt and whom do you need to ask to forgive you?
3. Ask God to forgive you, promising you intend never to do it again.
4. Now tear up the piece of paper – it's all over!
5. If you still feel guilty, find a wise friend, counsellor or minister to pray with you and help you.

Reaction page

Take a moment to list things that you have done wrong and feel guilty about – these can be big or small things, they can be things you did years ago or just today.

Each time, after you have made a list, read Romans 8:1 and then decide what action is needed to remove the guilt you feel in your life for this situation.

Guilty action	Guilt cleanser	Action to be taken to remove the guilt
	Romans 8:1	
	Romans 8:1	
	Romans 8:1	
	Romans 8:1	
	Romans 8:1	
	Romans 8:1	

After you have worked through a way of dealing with your guilt, remember it should always start by taking the wrong you have done to Jesus. Romans 5:8 reminds us that Christ died for us when we were sinners. So we need to hand the sin that we have done over to Him and receive His forgiveness. Also remember – if you really mean you are sorry and will try not do it again, then to God you are 100 per cent forgiven and from that moment onwards he has removed the incident from his memory.

Sometimes, the guilt we have is so deep and so painful that it looks as if it will never leave us. Don't settle for that – find someone wise and experienced such as your Church minister or youth leader. If you don't feel confident with either of these people then find someone else who you feel will listen to you, give good advice and be able to pray with you and for you.

Think it through...

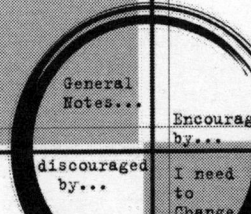

General Notes...
Encouraged by...
discouraged by...
I need to Change...

EVALUATE
✓ Get it RIGHT!

Honesty

The big issue

Taylor had a part-time job in a local supermarket. She worked after college from four o'clock to nine o'clock. It wasn't the most exciting job, but it paid money and that's why she did it. Recently, she had been promoted and was in charge of balancing the money in each of the tills at the end of the shift. Taylor didn't feel qualified to do it, but the extra money was great. She asked the manager why he had given her the job and he told her she was the only worker he could trust with the responsibility. The first day of her new role turned out to be a bigger headache than she had expected, as one of the tills was out by £50. The following day the same till was out by £30, the next day by £40, and by the end of the week that same till had miscalculated over £200.

The till was operated by a lady in her mid-forties called Margie. Taylor asked Margie why her till had been out each time. Margie said she must have scanned too many objects by mistake. Taylor made a note of this and adjusted the figures. However, the till continued to be out of money and eventually Taylor approached Margie for the truth. She replied without hesitation, 'Yeah okay I took it, but you want to know why? I'll tell you why. I have five kids – one of them is dying – he needs real care and that means big money. They want to put him in hospital but he won't be any better off. My husband is unemployed and basically unemployable. He's fifty years old, no real education and not the brightest of guys to talk to. I'm all the family's got to pin its hopes on, and they can't do that when I'm getting minimum wage. Give me a break!'

Taylor hadn't expected that kind of reply, she had no idea that Margie had the kind of problems she had described. The fact that her son was dying was just too much. She needed work and Taylor certainly wasn't going to deprive her of it. 'I'm sorry about your family, and I'm not going to tell the manager, but you have 2 choices – you either stop taking the money or you find another job that pays better.'

Margie agreed and went away with tears in her eyes. The following week Taylor was taken into the manager's office and told that money had gone missing when she was in charge – did she know anything about it? 'Yes, there have been a few computer errors, from my observations. I think it's been sorted.' The manager was happy with her answer and asked her to keep an eye out for staff stealing money from the tills.

Talking point

- Did Taylor lie to her boss, and if she did, was the lie justified?
- Taylor believed Margie's story. Would you be so quick to believe her?
- What would you have done if you had been in Taylor's shoes?
- Have you ever found yourself in that kind of position?
- Sometimes you know for sure that not telling the truth is by far the easier and better option all round. Do you think it's ever OK to play about with the truth if it means no-one will get found out or get into trouble? Yes or no? – give your reasons.
- By withholding information, Taylor had become party to a crime which in itself is a crime. Would you be willing to break the law for somebody else? If so, in what circumstances?

Bible point

James 5:12 – *'Above all my brothers and sisters, do not swear – not by heaven or by earth or by anything else. Let your "Yes" be yes, and your "No", no, or you will be condemned'*

If we stretch or fabricate the truth then in the end people will stop believing us – no one will trust us. To start playing with the truth is a very dangerous thing to do. So in other words make it real simple and tell the truth (let your 'Yes' be yes or 'No' be no) without any twists or stretches.

Proverbs 30:8 – *'Keep falsehood and lies far from me'*

If people give us false information or lie to us, and we believe them, we become part of something that is wrong. We need to protect ourselves from untruths, otherwise we ourselves will be spreading lies to others. Think twice before mixing with, and listening to, people whom you know continually lie or stretch the truth.

Micah 7:3 – *'Both hands are skilled in doing evil; the ruler demands gifts, the judge accepts bribes, the powerful dictate what they desire – they all conspire together'*
We live in a corrupt world where people get by in life by being dishonest and taking bribes ('You do me this favour and I'll get you what you want quicker/cheaper'). It's easy for us to become a part of this but such twisted thinking only damages the community we live in. Try and stay clear and resist getting pulled into these temptations.

Listening point

Here's a question for you! 'What has honesty got to do with stretching the truth a little bit?' Think about it for a minute, where would we be if we were expected to tell the exact truth with all its details every time something went wrong or someone got too nosey? We'd see more smashed-up faces and experience a good deal more hatred. Because if we go around telling everyone the truth about everything we will upset a lot of people and get a lot of people into trouble. That surely can't be right?

Take Abraham for example in the Bible – his wife was so attractive that he was afraid somebody might kill *him* to get *her*. So he lied so as to save his life – he said she was his sister. Was Abraham wrong?

Unlike his great grandad Abraham, when Joseph was totally honest, everything went wrong for him. He was a real stunner and his boss's wife wanted to sleep with him. When Joseph said, 'No!' she understandably got upset and told a different version of events to her husband so poor whiter-than-white Joseph ended up in prison. What good did his honesty do him?

So perhaps we need to learn discretion – there is a time to tell the truth, a time to twist it and a time to avoid it all together, right? Well, life would certainly be interesting if things worked out that way, but God doesn't like that approach. He prefers straight and simple honesty, which in other words means telling the truth, being just and fair and not trying to rip others off in life. 'Why?' you may well ask, 'That doesn't seem very sensible'. It just depends how you look at it. For every lie you tell, you normally have to tell another one to support the previous one. One simple lie could require twenty more to give credit to your first lie. The end result may in some cases get you out of trouble, but in others it could dig you a hole so deep that you will never get out of it. Abraham didn't benefit from telling the world he wasn't married to his wife. He was found out and people didn't trust him afterwards. In fact, people didn't want to know him at all, they hated him. Joseph, on the other hand, became successful by being honest and not cheating on his boss. Prison wasn't nice but what happened in prison brought him fame, success and wealth. Had he been dishonest, things would have ended very differently. Pretending may cover up a whole load of embarrassing things, but the truth has a habit of escaping at some time or another! An affair may seem out of the question for you, just like it did for Joseph, but have you never been tempted to brag falsely, or 'forget' to pay for something, or make yourself feel better by telling lies about someone else?

There comes a time when being dishonest, cheating or deceiving someone can seem really attractive. It may get you out of a tough corner or make you look a little better for a moment. But it's never a good move to be anything other than honest. The Bible says 'A false witness will not go unpunished, and he who pours out lies will not go free' (Proverbs 19:5). And Jesus said that it's 'the truth [which] will set you free' (John 8:32). Be free, life's a lot less complicated that way, and you will be a great example to others who watch you to see how you live your life as a Christian!

Radical Action Guide

Before you speak, ask yourself:
1. Is what I am about to say the entire truth?
2. Is what I am about to say stretched in any way?
3. Does what I am about to say conveniently leave an important piece of information?
4. By not talking or by my actions could I be deliberately deceiving someone?
5. Do I hang around people who are known for lying or being economical with the truth? Do I let them influence me?
6. Always, when facing an honesty challenge, make a conscious decision to check yourself by asking each of the five questions above. Be brave, be strong and be honest!

Honesty Scales

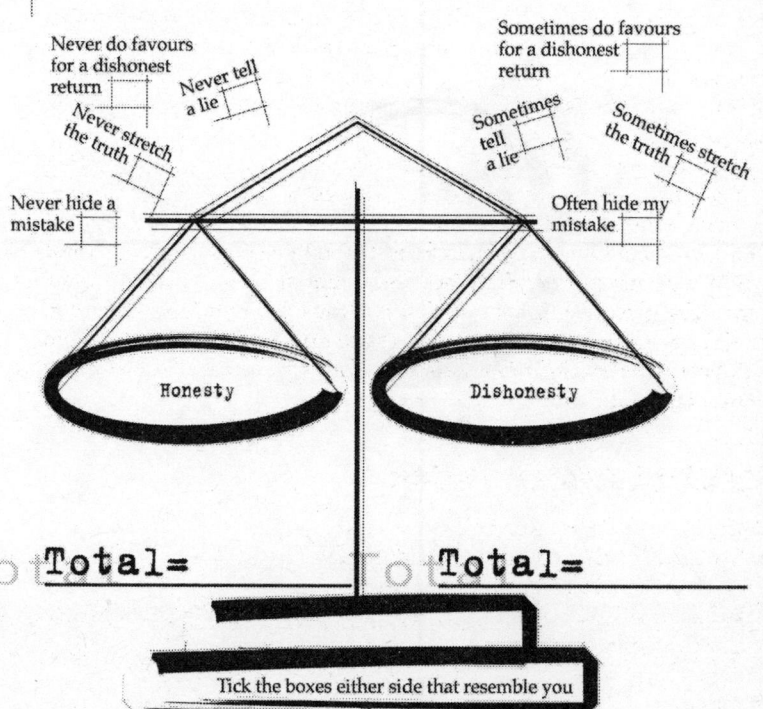

Tick the boxes either side that resemble you

Think it through...

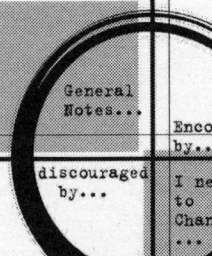

General Notes...

Encouraged by...

discouraged by...

I need to Change...

EVALUATE

✓ Get it RIGHT!

Identity

The big issue

John had always been good at sports and everyone around him knew it. His house was like a museum with trophies and cups stacked up wherever space allowed, and if someone failed to notice them there were always the pictures hanging on the wall showing him with a medal round his neck or newspaper cuttings with John shaking some unknown official's hand.

John was good at everything, but he was exceptional at football. When he was just fifteen, a scout from a Premier Division club had tried to sign him up. He was never short of friends and never seemed to have problems finding a girlfriend. Everyone knew John was probably going to be famous one day. He was special! That was until John broke his leg on a school skiing trip. 'It's just a break,' he told himself as he was airlifted off the mountain by helicopter, but the doctors who looked at the x-ray at the nearby hospital could see it was far more serious than a break. In fact, he would be lucky ever to walk again on that leg. John did walk again but not without a limp and rarely without a stick. The scouts stopped calling, and John began to change. He wasn't the cool, exciting warm and friendly guy everyone in the school had known him to be. He became grumpy and unpredictable, at times completely unapproachable, hot tempered and unreasonable. Most of his friends gave up mainly because they didn't understand him any more. He was still hot property among the girls, but there was no queue – after all, who wants to date an attractive thorn bush?! A year later John flunked his exams, dropped out of school and went on the dole for two years. He ended up with a part-time job operating a photocopier for a small business.

Talking point

- How do you think John felt before his accident?
- How do you think he must have felt after his accident?

- Have you ever felt like John must have felt – either before or after his accident?

- The identity quiz

How popular do I feel I am?	Low 1 2 3 4 5 High
How secure do I feel in myself?	Low 1 2 3 4 5 High
How secure do I feel in how others view me?	Low 1 2 3 4 5 High
How much of my happiness comes from what I do well?	Low 1 2 3 4 5 High
How much of my happiness comes from what others think I do well?	Low 1 2 3 4 5 High
How much of the time do I really enjoy my life?	Low 1 2 3 4 5 High

- How important is it to you what other people think and feel about you. Why?

- John's biggest problem was not the breaking of his leg but dealing with the changes in his life. If you had been John what would you have done to try and get back on top of life again?

- If someone asked you to describe who you are, what would you say?

Bible point

Who am I as a Christian? *I am a child of God (John 1:12).*
I am loved by God and nothing can ever change that (Romans 8:39).
I am able to do everything through Jesus (Philippians 4:13).
I am somebody who has been chosen by God and adopted into his family (Ephesians 1:5).
I am a temple of the Holy Spirit (1 Corinthians 6:19).
I am worth dying for (Romans 5:8).
I am a light in the world (Matthew 5:14).

What do I have as a Christian? *I have freedom (Galatians 5:1).*
I have forgiveness (1 John 1:9).
I have no reason to be condemned (Romans 8:1).
I have been given a place with Jesus in heaven (Ephesians 2:6).
I have citizenship in heaven (Ephesians 2:19).

> *I have the inheritance that God gives to his children (Galatians 4:7).*
> *I have the Holy Spirit (1 Corinthians 12:3).*

Listening point

Everybody wants to be somebody, right? You don't hear many people saying they want to be poor, unknown, unloved and unimportant! Have you ever met a man with a mysterious female name tattooed on his arm? 'Who's Sandra?' you ask, only to be told it's the name of a girl he went out with three years ago. Why would anyone do that? Well, either because they were drunk at the time or because they would do anything to be accepted by someone else.

But what makes someone accepted? Is it being cool, one of the lads, having lots of money, great clothes, or being good at something? That's how it had been for John – at least until the accident. But John had misunderstood what being 'somebody' was about. He thought it was to do with success and potential fame – it never occurred to him that people liked him because of who he was. He could have been the greatest footballer who ever lived but still have no friends; people liked John because first and foremost he was a great guy. The problem was not the accident, it was his own understanding of his identity. He thought talent equalled success, fame and popularity, ultimately resulting in the status of being 'somebody'! But this couldn't have been further from the truth. His friends were still there as much after the accident as they were before – sure the football scouts had lost interest, but that was all! He wasn't destined for fame any more and he wouldn't earn the wonderful salary he might have had, but he was still the same person. His greatest loss was his belief in himself which had been based upon what the world teaches.

So what does the world teach us? It teaches us that in order to be someone we need ten straight A GCSE's, at least three A levels and a degree from a good university. We need to look really good, be athletic, blonde and busty if you're a girl, tough and able to take care of yourself if you're a guy, be able to down five pints of beer in a night, and to have had sex at least once by year 11 at school. After finishing at uni you should have a well-paid job, a good car, a big house, take international holidays, and have plenty of money in the bank for rainy days.

But what happens if you don't achieve what the world tells you is important, or if you wake up one morning and realise you don't want to be the person you are becoming? What happens if you can't get the grades at school, or you can't be as slim or as tough as you'd like? You become like John, a confused nobody who was once a potential somebody. But you only become like that if you think like that!

Jesus said that if you belong to the world it will love you as its own (John 15:19). If you are a Christian, then you do not belong to the world. The world's standards aren't the same as yours, its pressures don't need to be as tough for you. Yes, you live in the world but you now belong to God – you are completely his. Does it matter if you don't get a starting salary of £50,000 a year, or you only got one A level instead of three? Yes it does, if you only care about what other people think. But if you are more concerned about what God thinks, then things are very different. You see, he loves you regardless of whether you're a somebody or not, and he has plans for your life that are more exciting than you could ever dream of, whether you have a degree or you leave school at sixteen. Formal education is extremely important, don't misunderstand me. But get things into perspective. His plans for you far outweigh the success you could ever achieve in life on your own – based on school, college or university results.

Take another look at your answers to the identity quiz and the question 'If someone asked you to describe who you are what would you say?' Do you care more than anything else about what other people think? Have you become a clone of people's expectations, or do you base your value and identity on what God wants of you and what he thinks about you? If you don't know who you are, then look again at the Bible point, because you are someone very special. In fact, you are an amazing person with such a lot going for you and with a great future ahead of you! Don't rely on what other people think or what they want you to be like, nor even on what you think or want, like John did. But rely on God and his viewpoint – you're a far better person with him than you are with anyone else!

Radical Action Guide

1. Take a look at your life, and work out whom you ultimately live to please (yourself, others, God).
2. If you are more concerned about what you perceive others think rather than what God thinks about you, then ask yourself why?
3. With that answer read John 1:12 and Ephesians 1:5 and ask who is the most important to you, others or God?
4. Seek out a friend who will pray, encourage you and check your motives, on a regular basis, as to why you do things the way you do.
5. Remind yourself daily that God loves you, has a plan for you, has many things to give so he can help you and has a place in heaven ready for you. Take your value from him and watch everything else take second place!

Reaction Page

When I decide on …	Am I trying to please Myself?	Others?	God?
The clothes I wear			
My haircut			
The fragrance I wear (aftershave/perfume)			
My weight and figure			
The way I talk, the words I use, the stories I tell			
The food I eat			
The way I choose my friends			
The things I do with my friends			
The way I relax (cinema/pub/TV)			
The girl or boyfriends I look for			
The things I do with my girl or boyfriends			
How hard I study at school/college			
The things I do at school/college			
The reason I go to church or youth fellowship group			
The way I spend my money			
The things I do at home			
The help I give or don't give at home			
My part or full-time job			
The exercise I do or don't do			

Take a moment to think about these questions after looking at the above chart.
1. Am I my own person? Why? Why not?
2. Do I enjoy life?
3. Am I comfortable with failure? Why? Why not?
4. Am I comfortable with how other people view me? Why? Why not?
5. Do I ultimately live to please myself, others or God?

Think it through...

- General Notes...
- Encouraged by...
- discouraged by...
- I need to Change...

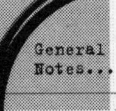

EVALUATE

✓ Get it RIGHT!

Judging

The big issue

Every evening Jonathan would spend at least three or four hours on his computer. His parents said he was being anti-social, because he watched a computer screen all night. 'On the contrary,' he replied, and told them he was on a chat line. Over the six months he used the line he came across literally hundreds of people, however there was one particular person, named Sam, with whom he communicated more often than with anyone else. Each night, Jonathan would connect up and wait anxiously for Sam to sign on, then the two of them would type messages back and forth. Jonathan found Sam to be so similar, they liked the same kind of sports, supported the same teams, hated school, liked fast food. Similar height, age, and from what Sam wrote, they had a similar dress sense. Jonathan finally suggested that they meet each other. Sam agreed. They set a time and place. Jonathan was there early, but Sam didn't show up on time. In fact Sam didn't show up at all. That evening Jonathan wrote to his chatmate asking why he hadn't turned up. To Jonathan's surprise Sam asked exactly the same question, claiming to have waited over two hours for Jonathan. They set a new time and place. Jonathan double-checked the details before leaving. He arrived early, but again there was no sign of Sam. Thirty minutes went by, still no sign. There was another person waiting over the road, but it wasn't Sam. However, strangely enough, he remembered that same person had been there last time. The other person glanced over, their eyes met, and the person began to cross the road. Jonathan had no idea who it was, and didn't really care to find out. The person approached. 'Hi!' Jonathan said, a little bit embarrassed. The person replied, 'I'm Sam!' Jonathan couldn't quite take it in. 'You must be Sam?' Jonathan asked. 'Err, yeah that's right.' Sam sensed Jonathan's surprise, 'so, what is it you didn't expect, that I'm a girl or that I'm black?'

Talking point

- What the story didn't say was that Jonathan was a male and white. You, however, may or may not have assumed that he was, or wasn't. Jonathan had not expected Sam to be a girl or black. Why do you think you – and Jonathan – made these assumptions?

- Was Jonathan in any way sexist or racist for assuming Sam was the same sex and colour?

- Have you ever made an assumption about what somebody would be like before meeting them, only to find out they are entirely different?

- In what other ways do we make judgments about people?

- Has anyone ever made a wrong judgment about you? How did you feel?

- We often make judgments about people we know but we especially make judgments about people we don't know so well. Often our judgment can be harsh, cruel and unfair. Most of the time judging other people is wrong. When in your opinion is it right?

- 'Wow, he is so fit!' or 'She is one hot babe!' Are these two statements judgments or informed opinions based on your view of how attractive someone looks?

- If the person is not attractive are you less likely to want to know them? If so, have you judged them on their appearance and not on their character?

Bible point

2 Chronicles 19:7 – *'Now let the fear of the Lord be upon you. Judge carefully, for with the Lord our God there is no injustice or partiality or bribery'*
These were the instructions King David gave to the men he chose to serve as judges. Well, you might not be a legal judge, but you do have common sense. Be sure to judge with an open mind, don't sit back if things are wrong. But be fair, and make sure your actions are like Jesus because he is the one you represent!

Isaiah 11:3,4 – *'He will not judge by what he sees with his eyes, or decide by what he hears with his ears; but with righteousness he will judge the needy, with justice he will give decisions for the poor of the earth'*

This is how Isaiah describes the ideal King. You probably hate it when someone makes a judgment about you because of how you look or talk. But often we do that to others, whether we intend to or not. Jesus is the only one who can look and listen to people and not judge on appearance or manners. He looks beyond into their hearts. However that's not an adequate excuse for us. Because we are Christians, Jesus lives in us and given time, our own reactions and judgments should slowly begin to change to be more like his. Make sure that you are doing everything possible to let Jesus change you.

John 8:7 – *'If any one of you is without sin, let him be the first to throw a stone at her'*

A group of religious leaders took a woman who had committed adultery and dragged her before Jesus. They were shouting that the law stated she should be killed. But Jesus did not judge her and before he would let anyone else do so, he insisted that they first judge themselves. Before we speak an idle word or dwell on a judgmental thought, we should do what Jesus urged the leaders of the law to do and ask ourselves whether we are perfect. If we aren't, then what right do we have to judge someone else?

Listening point

We make judgments all the time, in fact our brain works overtime making judgments. It's like a sixth sense, 'He looks an idiot!', 'I wouldn't trust her, anyone who wears make-up like that should be locked away!', 'He must be one of those weird boffins because he watches the news – he probably wears a raincoat and does the crossword as well!', 'He's definitely a train spotter, just look at his glasses!', 'She must be gay!', 'He'll never get a girlfriend, who would want him?', 'She'll never pass her driving test, she's hopeless at everything!' Some of the things we say sound funny and can get a laugh but they are also often very cruel and in most cases completely untrue. But what do we care? – it gets a smile, and judging people can be a favourite recreation – forget football, clubbing or getting legless. A little huddle, an easy target, and the race is on to see who can come up with the best judgment on the geek in the corner. Jimmy wins for reckoning the geek has three nipples and stores pictures of hamsters in his pocket. But often what we say about others is what we recognise in ourselves and would love to change.

Perhaps you don't have three nipples or love hamsters but there may well be other things you'd like to hide. It's easy to highlight someone else's faults while secretly trying to cover up your own. What did you do when you were about seven or eight years old in the playground and someone would say something horrible about you like, 'Four eyes, get real glasses instead of jam jars!'? Apart from wanting to sever their head with a chain saw, you most probably diverted attention by saying something just as nasty about someone else. As we grow older, we still make wild statements, true or false, but we become much better at hiding what we do. Jesus says, 'Do not judge, or you too will be judged' (Matthew 7:1). It's certainly true that the more you judge people, the more people judge you for judging them, but the Bible didn't mean that. It meant that God will judge you. How people live their lives, dress, walk, talk, or look, may seem very odd or just downright stupid, but we should zip our mouths and divert our thoughts. In other words, the Bible tells us to mind our own business. Anyhow, the definition of 'odd' or 'strange' is often anyone different from yourself. Which means that while you may be a cool dude or trendsetter, to someone else you are 'odd'. That's not a nice thought, but the thoughts you have about other people may not be nice either. Take Jesus' advice – 'Do to others what you would have them do to you!' (Matthew 7:12). Being totally blunt, don't judge, make assumptions, be horrible or gossip about anyone unless you want them to do the same to you!

This advice may seem a bit hard and likely to take the fun out of life. But the Bible does give two occasions for judgment. The first is that Christians should judge the actions of other *Christians* who keep doing wrong stuff (1 Corinthians 5:12). Now don't go crazy here and start making a list of every sin any Christian you know has committed, that is not what it means. Nor does it mean we can poke a finger and smugly say 'Who's a naughty Christian then?' Judging doesn't mean we stop being helpful, constructive, and loving. For example, one of your church mates does something wrong, like lying. You can do one of two things: you might tell him in front of everyone he is a liar and shouldn't be trusted. Or you could take him aside and gently say, 'I heard what you said. You probably didn't realize what you did was wrong but perhaps you should go back and change things?' Don't accuse, but help him or her to get the problem sorted out and to get right with God again. To embarrass or try to rule over someone is never right, and our actions will not please God. Remember Jesus also said, 'Take the plank out of your own eye, and then you will see clearly to remove the speck from your brother's eye' (Matthew 7:5). In other words, don't be a hypocrite and don't be self-righteous.

The second occasion for judgment in the Bible gives us room for using common sense to judge wrong things done by any one, especially when others are being hurt by it. The Bible certainly doesn't expect us to sit back and say, 'Sorry, I'm not allowed to judge that using a cricket bat to squash another person's head is wrong. And even if I am, I'm not perfect, so carry on.' Get in there and sort it out!

One last thing. Jonathan made a big assumption about Sam. It was based on his own background. Ask yourself what's the best way to handle the problem. Our first impressions of people are often wrong. Jonathan was neither racist nor sexist. He just happened to be a male, who was white and living in a completely white neighbourhood. He was, however, small-minded to think Sam would be a clone of himself. Generally, we expect or want people to be just like us – but if we do that we limit our world and miss out on so much. If we break out of that mould then we enjoy life so much more. Jonathan quickly shrugged off his wrong assumption and the two of them ended up dating! Do whatever it takes to stop judging, because if you do you will enjoy life in a wholly different way. You can have a friendship without feeling guilty for what you thought or did and also there are going to be fewer people out there saying ridiculous rubbish about you!

Radical Action Guide

Before you make a judgment about someone else, be sure to ask the following questions:
1. Does it matter?
2. Is it true?
3. Am I perfect?
4. Will whatever I think, say or do be helpful to that person?
5. Will Jesus be pleased if I get involved, or would he prefer I just minded my own business?

Judgment Glasses

Whenever we judge a person we usually do so for one of two reasons - because they are strange, or have done something strange, or because they have done something wrong.

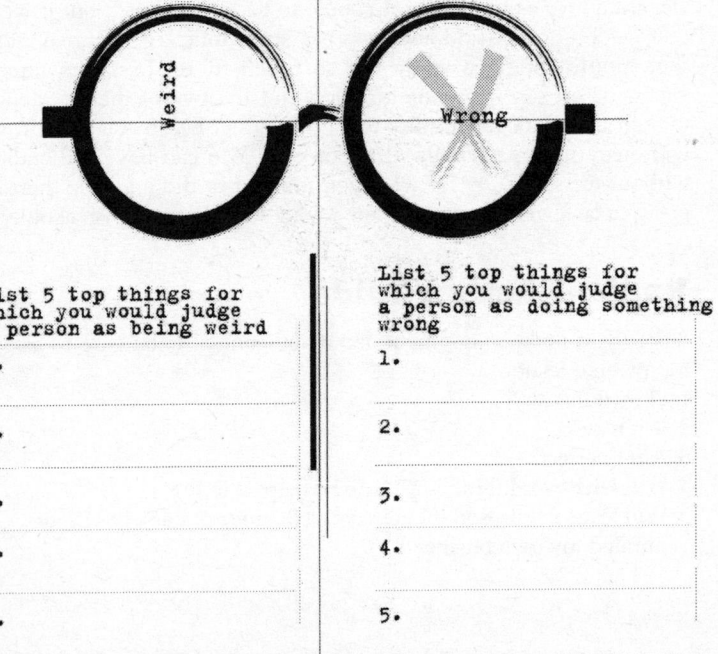

List 5 top things for which you would judge a person as being weird

1.
2.
3.
4.
5.

List 5 top things for which you would judge a person as doing something wrong

1.
2.
3.
4.
5.

From your list of 10, take a moment to answer which of the top 10, if any, are ever right for you to judge another person by? and what, if any, action should you take?

Are you able to judge a person as Christ would judge you?
If not, what needs to change so that you can?

Think it through...

- General Notes...
- Encouraged by...
- discouraged by...
- I need to Change...

EVALUATE

✓ Get it RIGHT!

Kindness

The big issue

Claire had waited two years for this chance. She had been selected to model designer clothes for a top show in London. She had worked hard on her figure and just as hard at getting herself chosen. That day Claire had given herself plenty of time to get to the hall, but she didn't know the city very well at all and with her poor sense of direction she needed the extra time. From the tube station the hall was less than three hundred metres away, but as she came out of the tube and turned in the direction she was supposed to be going in, engrossed in her map, she didn't see the motionless body sprawled out on the floor and tripped over it.

She quickly picked herself up off the pavement and turned in anger to see what had caused her to fall. At first she was horrified to find out it was a body, but her concern soon turned to disgust as she discerned the body was that of a no-good drunk. 'Get up and get a life!' she said flippantly, not expecting a reply. As she began to walk in the general direction in which she was supposed to be going, the young model heard a voice asking for help. It was the drunk. 'Help, you don't need help!' she retorted, 'you need discipline and will-power!' Looking at her watch Claire was about to turn away, for she would soon be late, but again the body asked for help. This time the tramp moved and a young girl's face appeared from behind the blankets and overcoat.

'How old are you?' Claire asked in shock, hesitating – she couldn't be much older than twelve. The girl didn't look well at all, her face was pale and the puddle of vomit next to her hadn't escaped Claire's attention. Kneeling down next to her, she knew the girl needed medical help without delay. As she began to think about what to do the thought of the fashion show suddenly brought her back to reality. She couldn't stay and help her. If she did, she would miss the show and her career would be over before it started. With that, Claire took her leave, shouting over her shoulder that she would phone for an ambulance from the show. The girl was left alone groaning in the street.

Talking point

- What would you have done if you had been Claire?
- Have you ever been caught in a situation where someone needed your help but you had other things you wanted or needed to do? What happened?
- What were Claire's options and which do you think was the right option to take?
- Is there a line between being kind and being soft or being walked over? If you think there is, where do you think the line should be drawn? (give examples).
- Have you ever been in a situation when you needed someone else's help, but you knew the person didn't want to help or your need was just too demanding for them? What happened?

Bible point

Kindness is a sign of the Holy Spirit in your life.	'The fruit of the Spirit is love, joy, peace, patience, kindness, goodness, faithfulness, gentleness, and self control' Galatians 5:22–23
Kindness is a demonstration of your love for Jesus.	'Whatever you did for one of the least of these brothers and sisters of mine, you did for me' Matt 25:40
Kindness may involve sacrifice and personal discomfort.	' ... If someone strikes you on the right cheek, turn the other also. And if someone wants to sue you and take your tunic hand over your cloak as well. If someone forces you to go one mile, go two miles. Give to the one who asks you, and do not turn away from the one who wants to borrow from you' Matt 5:39-42

Listening point

Kindness is one of those irritating words that whines around your head like a bloodthirsty mosquito at the moment you are about to fall asleep. You get on the bus after a long hard day at school or work, you feel exhausted and there is just one seat left. You take it, and you begin to melt into the cushion. The world slowly disappears, but just before you leave planet earth your eyes fix on an old woman, with shopping bag in one hand and stick in the other fumbling up the aisle, squinting the entire way trying to locate a seat. There are no seats left – you took it!

Or what about when you head for the canteen at lunchtime and take the last chocolate milk shake, only to hear some poor guy behind you moaning that there are no more left and they'd been dreaming of one all morning? Guilt smacks you in the face. 'So what are you, selfish or kind?' Your conscience shrieks. 'Have my seat', or 'have this drink', you say with a smile on your face while every bit of you inside is thinking unrepeatable thoughts. Most of us have learned what it means to pretend to be nice and kind. You can look good if you have to, but you don't really have to mean it. If it saves someone else being hurt or upset, or if it means you need to play your part in society's expectations of politeness then you will do your little bit! And that's great, because Jesus wants us to be like that, but the thing about Jesus is that he often wants that bit more from us than we are willing to give.

Jesus wants our kindness to be built on more than just guilt or social conformity – he wants it to be built on love. Look again at the passage in Matthew 5:39–42 which mentions turning the other cheek or going the extra mile. Kindness, in Jesus' view, goes beyond politeness and social standards. It's being nice even when people are being horrible. If the old dear on the bus had pulled you by the hair and said, 'Get up you little piece of dirt!' or the guy in the canteen had smacked you in the ribs and taken the milkshake out of your hand, you might not have been so generous. The old lady might have found herself sitting down, but not in your seat, more likely on the floor with her shopping bag on her head! And if the guy who wanted the milkshake had been rude, he most likely would have ended up with it down his throat! 'Kindness has its limits', right? Well actually, no, it doesn't, but we do.

The kindness Jesus talked about and showed us was a kindness without limit – it was a love that required effort and action. Claire was probably doing what most people would do, helping the girl while still pursuing her career. But the kindness Jesus refers to is one of sacrifice. Jesus wouldn't have left the girl for any selfish reason. He talked about denying oneself, and placing others first (Matthew 20:26–28). The story is like the one that Jesus told about the 'Good Samaritan' (Luke 10:30-35). A Samaritan would have been the least likely to help a Jew, but he did, and he gave beyond measure. In this world there are lots of people who don't know Jesus, yet in what they do, they appear to be better Christians than we are. They offer help to people no one else wants to help and they give their time when they could be doing far more enjoyable things. Yet you and I have the Holy Spirit living in us, and part of the sign of his presence in our lives is the 'kindness' we show. How kind are you? Don't hold it back, and make sure when a person is in need you don't pass them by.

Radical Action Guide

1. Always be on the lookout for the opportunity to be kind.
2. Be willing to be kind, knowing you may get nothing in return.
3. Be kind even if the person isn't very nice.
4. Be kind even when there is no good reason why you should be.
5. Be kind beyond what other people would expect of you.
6. Be kind even when you neither have the time nor the desire to make the effort.
7. Be kind when you are in a bad mood.
8. Be kind on the inside as well as the outside.

Kindness dilemma

You meet each of these 3 people at the same time. Which of the three are you most likely to help?

Drop dead gorgeous girl or guy who lost his or her bus pass.

Class nerd, tripped over his desk, smashed his glasses and broke his nose

Your best mate who is looking for an excuse to get out of his next class

What made you choose the person you chose?

Is there any of these 3 people you wouldn't help? Why?

Is there anyone or any situation that you would never offer help to, if help was needed? Why?

Does reading Matthew 5:38-42 and Matthew 25:31-46 change your view in any way?

Think it through...

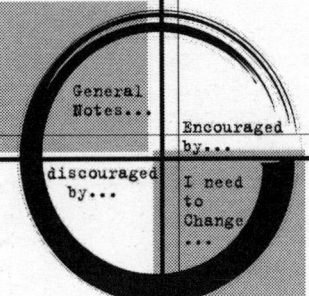

General Notes...
Encouraged by...
discouraged by...
I need to Change...

EVALUATE
✓ Get it RIGHT!

Love

The big issue

'She is really quite something!' Carl told his friends. He was referring to Rachel who had just joined the sixth form. Before Carl could say anything else, one of his mates screamed to Rachel at the top of his voice across the common room, repeating every word Carl had just said – with a few of his own explicit suggestions for good measure. The common room fell quiet, followed by a few jeers and laughs. Carl turned bright red and muttered under his breath how he would deal with his friend later.

At the end of the day, as he was leaving the school, he saw Rachel walking alone and took it as his chance to say 'Hi'. 'I'm sorry about my friend earlier – he really can be a jerk!' were his opening words to the girl, whom he was finding more and more attractive by the minute. 'Forget it!' she replied gently and turned away. Carl was growing in confidence, since he had now talked to her. He quickly caught up with Rachel again. 'Listen, I know how hard it must be for you being new, if you'd like I could show you round and introduce you to people?' She stopped and smiled. 'OK, why not? How about tonight?' They made plans and Carl left very excited – he had a date with the hottest girl in the school.

Before meeting with her later, Carl had a shower, shaved, found some of his dad's aftershave that he later decided smelt repulsive, and pulled out the clothes that he thought made him most irresistible. As they had agreed, Carl met Rachel outside the railway station. She looked great – apparently she had made a real effort too. Carl was feeling very optimistic about how things were going. 'Hi Carl,' Rachel said, and then turned to a person behind her 'this is Oliver, my boyfriend. I met him a couple of weeks back. He is new to the area too, so if it's OK you can show us both around.'

Talking point

- How do you think Carl would feel when meeting Rachel's boyfriend?

- Carl found Rachel really attractive. What does it mean to be attracted to someone?

- What's the difference between feeling 'something' for someone and love?

- Describe the difference between the love you have for your dog, the love you have for your parents and being in love with a girl or boyfriend?

- Do you think being attracted to or being in love with someone is really a chemical reaction leading to the desire for sex?

- Do you think guys differ from girls when it comes to love? How?

Bible point

1 Corinthians 13:4-7 – *'Love is patient, love is kind. It does not envy, it does not boast, it is not proud. It is not rude, it is not self-seeking, it is not easily angered, it keeps no record of wrongs. Love does not delight in evil but rejoices with the truth. It always protects, always trusts, always hopes, always perseveres'*

If you have ever been to a Church wedding, then you are almost certain to have heard this passage. It kind of sums up what love is and how we should love someone. It's also one of the greatest instructions ever given on what we should or shouldn't do to have a great relationship with another person. Underlying this description of successful love is one word – 'sacrifice'.

2 Samuel 11:2,4 – *'One evening David got up from his bed and walked around on the roof of the palace. From the roof he saw a woman bathing. The woman was very beautiful ... Then David sent messengers to get her. She came to him and he slept with her'*

This is a story of romance, adultery and tragedy. David sees a woman (Bathsheba) who is the wife of another man (Uriah) and wants her. She becomes pregnant but it's obviously not her husband's child, for he is away, fighting a battle. David makes things even worse when he covers up his one night stand by killing Uriah. The baby is born but God's disapproves of all that David has done, and the baby dies. Right at the start, David was not in love with Bathsheba – he simply lusted for her and the outcome of his actions was disastrous. Love and lust are very different; the signs of love are described in 1 Corinthians 13, while this story describes the signs of lust. One is positive and constructive, the other negative and damaging.

Matthew 5:43,44 – *'You have heard that it was said, "Love your neighbour and hate your enemy". But I tell you: Love your enemies and pray for those who persecute you ...'*

The kind of love described in 1 Corinthians 13 isn't just confined to someone you want to go out with or marry, it isn't just for family and close friends. The love Jesus talks about is for anyone, even the people we don't like!

Listening point

Do you remember your first kiss? How could you forget? It was probably not how you imagined it would be – was it a bit gooey, slobbery, or dribbley, or did the other person nearly kill you with their breath? It could have been worse – you might have missed their mouth altogether or clashed braces (if you wear them that is)! For some people, however, their first kiss is like all the planets in the universe moving at once, stars falling and love bubbling! That's not love though, it's chemistry – hormones going wild together over an internal bunsen burner. It kind of sends you a bit crazy and makes you feel amazing but it ain't love!

So what is love? The English language is great, but sometimes it uses one word to cover lots of meanings. Love is one of those words – for example, you may love your hamster, your Levis, your sister, your dad and your boyfriend or girlfriend. But you don't love them all the same way, at least I hope not. You feel different feelings for each of them, right? Well, the New Testament is written in Greek and this is a language that uses different words for different kinds of love. Here's a peek at some of those words and meanings:

Philia – Love for your friends, something deep and special where loyalty is strong.
Storge – Affectionate love where sentiments are strong.
Eros – I am in LOVE! Where you are attracted to someone of the opposite sex and hold a strong physical bond.
Agape – A love that is demonstrated by actions, where you are willing to be sacrificial and lay aside your own needs or desires, a love even where you are prepared to die for another person.

The one true love!

So now we've got that sorted, let's get back to the love the world goes mad about, the 'falling in love', 'living together love', and 'let's get married love'. Well, whatever it is, it isn't based on feelings. You see, feelings come and go but love is something broader, deeper and richer. People who base their love lives, and ultimately their marriages, on feelings, pretty much have little left after seven or eight years. What they felt before and in the very early years of marriage was great chemistry, but if that's all, then the chemistry goes and partners quietly begin to look elsewhere. Love isn't sex either. Now don't get me wrong – people who love each other usually have great sex lives[1] but that is a sign of love rather than the reality itself. People who combine all the expressions of love in their relationship (*philia, storge, eros, agape*) are the ones who have a real foundation. They are the ones who, twenty years on, feel exactly the same way. Where friendship and loyalty are strong and where sentiment and affection are real, the chemistry and attraction are vibrant and commitment and selflessness are a priority. That's what true love is, but even such a love as this has its vulnerability and weaknesses. Relationships need more than all these qualities, they need to be spiritually active as well. What I mean is, God needs to be a part of each couple's relationship. The Bible says, 'a cord of three strands is not quickly broken' (Ecclesiastes 4:12). With *God* a part of the relationship between *him* and *her*, there is an added strength and help that keeps love very much alive!

So your heart beats a little faster when you see a chick or a hunk across the room. Your knees weaken, she or he's on your mind all the time – you want to be with them, you dream about one of those special kisses and the strong cuddles that go on and on. Is that love? No, but it's great and if things go well you never know, it could turn into love!

So how do you know when you are in love? Or if the person you are seeing is the one you should think about spending the rest of your life with? Some people brush the questions aside, saying, 'You will just *know*!' Other people think this is the sixty-four thousand dollar question and with the divorce rate as high as it is, the obvious conclusion would be, 'You can't know!' Well, I would disagree. I think everyone can reach the place where they do know for sure. When you have found the person who makes you feel so unbelievably good about yourself, when you are as attracted to them emotionally and socially as you are physically – in other words, you get a kick out of their company as much as you do by the hugs and other stuff that sure feel good,[2] you find yourself doing things that seem positively out of character. For example, you actually enjoy laying aside your own needs because you know it will make the other person happy. You begin to feel a part of you is missing when the two of you are not together, and it dawns on you that you actually enjoy their company more than you have enjoyed anyone else's in the world. You are slowly growing confident about the thought of commitment and long-term relationship. If you can acknowledge and yet overlook irritations, and if you desperately want to overcome difficulties, even if it means you lose out (but still keep going together), then you are almost certainly in love or on the verge of it.

The kind of physical, social, and certainly spiritual influence they are on you tells you whether they are the right person for you. Do they complement your own characteristics and bring a balance to your personality? Most important of all, what do you feel God is saying to you about this relationship? Do you feel comfortable and at peace with yourself, both in general and when you pray? Love and the right person almost always go together, but hot feelings and the wrong person spells 'disaster'!

Loving your neighbour

Don't forget, though, as in relationships, there are many kinds of love. The love you have for someone of the opposite sex is certainly different from the love you have for your parents, your friends, and the love you should have for almost everyone else. Regardless of how we feel about each person or the value we give to each sort of love, God has a universal standard for how we should love people. Here it is – 'This is how we know what love is: Jesus Christ laid down his life for us. And we ought to lay down our lives for one another' (1 John 3:16).

What?

Well, before you start making your will, what this verse is telling us is that the very route to love is complete and unconditional sacrifice. Love isn't a feeling, it isn't a reward scheme, it's a decision and a disciplined, controlled way of behaving. You may not want to help out around the home, you may not wish to be kind to some weirdo at school, college or work, you may not want to help out your mate who's in trouble for a moment of stupidity. But here is where love kicks into action. You make the decision to act regardless of the sacrifice involved, knowing there is nothing in return and that the other person is the only one to benefit. That is what it means to lay down our lives for others. It involves putting other people way before ourselves regardless of the cost. Jesus didn't jump onto the cross with excitement, because he felt good about dying that day. He did it in fear, experiencing pain at the highest and most excruciating level, but he chose to do it out of love for us.

That kind of love is known as *agape*, and for every person you meet or know, God expects you to love them with the same love that Jesus showed to everyone he ever encountered – the sacrificial *agape* love. The love you have for your future husband or wife, your parents, your friends, your next-door neighbour, the person you don't like so much and those who are starving several thousand miles away who keep appearing on your TV sets – you are required by God to 'lay down your life' for them! Not just once, or even once in a while, but every single day. Are you making that sacrificial radical decision regardless of how you feel, or are you loving selectively and conditionally? This love has no conditions; it has no limits and it involves pure sacrifice.

Radical Action Guide

Show your love to your girl or boyfriend, parents, brothers, sisters, friends, and those people you just can't stand, by:

1. Being patient.
2. Being kind.
3. Being content.
4. Being humble.
5. Being polite.
6. Being selfless.
7. Being calm.
8. Being forgetful of their mistakes.
9. Being truthful.
10. Offering protection, hope and commitment.

---

[1] See chapter on sex
[2] See chapter on sex

the Love Quest

Choose any from the list below for your top 10 in either column

Top 10 'I love someone' who is:		Top 10 'I don't love someone' who is:
1	Cute	1
2	Fun	2
3	Moody	3
	Nice & Kind	
4	Grumpy	4
5	Sexy	5
	Hurtful	
6	Strong	6
	Disrespectful	
7	Busty	7
	Tight fisted	
8	Gentle	8
	Ugly	
9	Generous	9
	Bad mouthed	
10	Smiley	10

Cheeky
Trendy
Talkative
Quiet
Geeky
Great body
Attractive
Fit
Unhealthy
Manky lips
Cool
Poor breath
Good cook
T.V. Slouch
Einstein
In love with self
Can't dance
Nobbly knees
Great eyes

Take the top 5 of each and place them in the boxes below, could you ever see yourself loving this kind of person?

The list above on the left is Mr or Mrs Perfect while the other list above on the right is Mr or Mrs Pits. But people generally are not one or the other, they have both great things about them and not so great

1	1
2	2
3	3
4	4
5	5

If you couldn't cope with this combination which one could you cope with? Start again by choosing 5 perfect qualities and 5 not so perfect qualities and see how you feel with this combination.

Think it through...

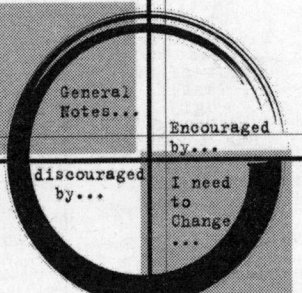

General Notes...
Encouraged by...
discouraged by...
I need to Change...

EVALUATE

✓ Get it RIGHT!

Money

The big issue

She had worked really hard for this first pay cheque. She had studied for five years at uni, and now Charlotte intended to celebrate with her money. Sure, she had a loan to start paying off, plus rent, utility bills – all needless to mention, after tax deductions, but she was going to have a great time. Charlotte had also decided that as a Christian she should give some of her earnings to a needy charity and to her Church.

The first night she and a couple of mates went into town, saw a movie and then ate at the local kebab house. Charlotte had told her friends that money was no object and she would pay! This is great, she thought, finally being able to do what she had always wanted. Plenty of freedom and lots of cash – she felt that at last she could live her life just as she had dreamed. Each night, Charlotte went out with different friends from work or old friends from school or university, and each time she paid the bill. After a week Charlotte realized she had spent almost all her money. The landlord wanted his cheque, the electricity and phone bill needed to be paid, there was no food in the house at all, and her car urgently needed new tyres and her bank balance wouldn't cover most of these things. Then she remembered she hadn't given anything to charity or to her Church. And she wouldn't get paid again for another three weeks.

Charlotte knew she had blown it and was facing having to take out a loan. Nothing would be going to charity now – in fact, she had turned into a pretty big charity case herself. Charlotte no longer felt so free and happy, but depressed and embarrassed for having been so easy with her money. If her parents found out, she would feel so small – like a child who had not yet grasped responsibility. She really didn't want that but she knew she deserved it.

Talking point

◆ What was Charlotte's biggest mistake with her money?

- Have you ever felt like Charlotte, knowing there are bills to be paid, people to be paid back and things to be bought, but you have already spent your money on more exciting alternatives?

- What kind of things do you spend your money on?

- Do you usually spend most of your money pretty soon after receiving it, or does it normally last until you next get paid?

- Where does your money come from? Do you have to work hard for it and are you paid fairly?

- Charlotte felt that as a Christian, she should give some of her money to her local Church and to charities. Is this something every Christian should do? Why?

- If Christians should give money to church or charities do you think it should be a percentage of their income, and if so how much?

- What does it feel like to be without money (and to owe people money)?

Bible point

Money doesn't make us happy.	*'Those who love money never have money enough; those who love wealth are never satisfied with their income. This too is meaningless'* Ecclesiastes 5:10.
We cannot love both God and money.	*'No one can be a slave to two masters. Either you will hate the one and love the other, or you will be devoted to the one and despise the other. You cannot serve both God and Money'* Matthew 6:24.
God and others should be more important to us than money.	*'Jesus answered, "If you want to be perfect, go, sell your possessions and give to the poor, and you will have treasure in heaven. Then come follow me"'* Matthew 19:21.
All our money belongs to God.	*'Calling the disciples to him, Jesus said, "I tell you the truth, this poor widow has put more into the treasury than all the others. They all gave out of their wealth; but she, out of her poverty, put in everything – all she had to live on"'* Mark 12:43–44.

Listening point

Most of us would do almost anything to have lots of money. We might not exactly want to be filthy rich, but a lot of dosh would be kind of cool! What else do people live for? As Christians we live for God, but we also live to make a few quid in life. We work hard in school, college or university for that glorious day when hard cash is handed over to us or put in our account. Let's face it, we don't work hard in order to be Mr or Mrs Struggle, who doesn't have a nice car, doesn't know if they can pay the mortgage or rent and can't feed or clothe the kids this month! We dream about being fitted out in life – top of the range car, large house, perfect wardrobe and the odd little luxury to make working worthwhile.

You know, there is nothing wrong with wanting any of these things. But there is something wrong when we want it more than we want God.

How can you ever tell that? Simple, here are a few questions for you to think about:

Do you have money on your mind a lot? Do you put off more important things so that you can make a couple of quid? Are you generous, and give to others to the point of it being a sacrifice and hurting, or do you seek your own needs first? Do God's plans get pushed aside because your thick wallet gives you alternative options? Are you wise in your spending? Are you quick to help others in need? Do you use your money to buy good things or bad things? Do you give your money to help in God's work? Are you in debt? Do you live to buy possessions, the latest clothing, and the things that 'everybody' simply 'must have'? These are just a few examples to help us check whether money, rather than God, is actually the main interest in our life. In fact money should not be anywhere near God on your list of priorities. The Bible is clear that we cannot serve both God and money (Matthew 6:24). For many people, money is actually their god – is it yours?

Confused? Let's try to get a handle on this. Jesus says two pretty hard-hitting things about money:
1. We should sell everything we own and give to the poor (Matthew 19:21).
2. It's very hard for the rich to enter the kingdom of God (Mark 10:23).

Wow?! That makes being a Christian impossible, because you're either poor with nothing, or you're not a member of the believers' club. But that probably doesn't ring true for you, when you see that most Christians (in the West at least) are not poor – they have lots of possessions. So are they disobedient, is Jesus not happy with them, are they actually heading for hell? No, not at all.

God expects us to be responsible with the money we have, we should take care of our needs such as eating, clothing and paying for the roof over our head. He doesn't even have a problem with extra stuff that you enjoy doing, but, and it's a big 'but', as a Christian, *everything you own (including your cash) belongs to God*. Therefore he doesn't expect you to be selfish or foolish with it – he doesn't expect you to ignore people in need. Nor does he expect you to be like Charlotte who spent all her money on fun stuff, but couldn't pay her way in life or help others out. And there's another: because you belong to God, at any point God may ask you to give away either your money or possessions to someone or something else. Hold everything loosely because it's not yours to hold on to! Even though, as we have discovered, everything belongs to God, he has put you in charge of managing his things, therefore be wise and careful and always willing to give.

What and how much should you give? The Bible talks about people giving away a percentage of what they earn – this is called tithing. 'Be sure to set aside a tenth of all that your fields produce each year'(Deuteronomy 14:22). Today, most of us don't own fields, but back then, crops were cash. What it means today is make sure God has a percentage of your income, at least 10 per cent.

Giving to God reminds us that he has provided us with work and he must be our priority in life. However we come back to the 'but'. The fact that we have given 10 per cent does not mean we don't have to give any more. God owns our pay cheque and that means we need to think hard before we go out and spend it on the latest computer game, clothes, or CD. The one thing you can be sure of is that God will not expect you to give all your dosh away without first taking care of your own needs, such as paying off the required monthly student loan or any bills you may be faced with. Be wise also in what you give to, don't just give away your money without any real knowledge of what will happen to it. Pray and ask God what he wants you to give to. Things like your Church, missionaries and charities are what Christians give to most, but he may have something very different in mind for you.

Jesus said that it's better to give than to receive (Acts 20:35), and he's actually right, because when we give we do receive. We are blessed from God, we receive a sense of fulfilment that our money is helping someone or something else and we receive joy because our action has pleased him.

Don't get hung up on money and don't be scared to give even if it makes your balance dip a little. Why? Because Jesus says he will provide all our needs according to his glorious riches (Philippians 4:19) and believe me, Jesus is very, very rich! So whether you earn £5 or £5000 a month, make sure you give, even if your giving seems small. Remember the story of the widow who gave only a tiny coin, but it was far more than anyone else's because it was all she had (Mark 12:41–44). Jesus doesn't measure the cash, he measures the effort and the sacrifice that giving takes.

Look after your money, use it wisely, stay out of debt. Enjoy your money, but be sure never to hold back from blessing others and blessing God with what he has blessed you!

Radical Action Plan

There's nothing wrong with using money for your own enjoyment, but make sure you:
1. Give your tithe.
2. Pay your bills and debts.
3. Use it wisely.
4. Have enough to see you through to your next pay day.
5. Use it for good and not bad.
6. Use it to bless others in need.
7. Don't allow it to become your main focus.
8. Hold it lightly.
9. Remember where it came from.
10. Don't announce to the world when and how you give.

how do you spend your money

Take a look at the cheque and place in your details of how much you receive each week or month from work, loans or pocket money. Then distribute your money into the various categories which reflect your current spending

- DVD/CD/Videos/Games
- Rent or lodging
- Electricity
- Phone Bill
- Clubs

The International Gold Bank   DATE: / /

Pay: _____

The sum of: _____

Cheque number 10810   Signature

1234567890

- Transportation
- Internet
- Clothing
- Movies
- Food
- Eating out
- Sports activities
- Tithe
- Other

Reflect - Do you think you spend your money wisely? Do you think God is pleased with how you spend your money?

If your income were to be reduced by half, what changes would you make in the above?

If your income were doubled, what changes would you make above?

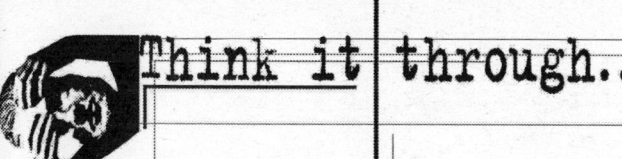
Think it through...

- General Notes...
- Encouraged by...
- discouraged by...
- I need to Change...

EVALUATE
✓ Get it RIGHT!

Needs

The big issue

'Just butt out, you Jesus freak!' Daniel yelled at Hannah across the classroom. Daniel was in his last year at school and he was well known for being a complete idiot. He was tall, well-built, and spent most of his life punching other people's brains out, while his own brains had been knocked back and forth to the point of resembling and operating like a scrambled egg. 'Intelligent' was not a word many people would have used to describe Daniel. Hannah was the exact opposite of Daniel – small, clever, articulate, and although she too had a reputation, it was because she, unlike Daniel, was a so-called 'born again' Christian.

'Listen, Dan, we all know what kind of trouble you are in and I just want to help' she retorted across the tables.

'What trouble am I in?' he growled at her with a grimace that offered more of a challenge than a question.

'You are a hurting person, you are never happy. You live in a children's home and you think the only way to work through your problems is by busting heads.' Her tone and sheer bravery shocked both Daniel and the rest of the class. 'What you need Dan ... ' Hannah was on a roll, but hesitated for a moment as she realized everyone in the class was now listening, including the teacher. She softened her voice and looked uncomfortable: 'What you need to know is that God loves you'.

Her comments dropped to the floor like clashing cymbals. Half the class burst out laughing while the other half opened their mouths in disbelief and embarrassment. As for Daniel, he stood up, grabbed a chair, raised it above his head, and catapulted his arms forward expecting the chair to hit the little Bible basher straight on the head. However, the chair did not move as the six-foot geography teacher gripped one of the legs. Hannah didn't even blink at the prospect of a large metal object flattening her to the ground. 'Daniel, I will love you no matter what you throw at me because Jesus told me to love even my enemies!'

Talking point

◆ Which of the following do you agree with, and why?

Hannah identified Daniel's problems and gave him the solution in a constructive manner.

Hannah identified Daniel's problems but did not give a solution in a constructive manner.

Hannah did not identify Daniel's problems but gave a solution in a constructive manner.

Hannah did not identify Daniel's problems and did not give a solution in a constructive manner.

◆ If you had been Hannah and had wanted to help Daniel work through his problems, recognizing he had both hurts and needs what would you have done?

◆ How would your approach differ from Hannah's?

◆ What do you think is a young person's biggest need?

◆ Can your faith help in meeting that need?

◆ In what ways can you reach out and help people in need? Think about the needs of the mind and body, as well as social and spiritual needs (Luke 2:52).

	Mind	Body	Social	Spiritual
1.				
2.				
3.				

Bible point

Luke 10:27 – *Jesus answered, 'Love the Lord your God with all your heart and with all your soul and with all your strength and with all your mind', and, 'Love your neighbour as yourself'*

That's certainly a lot of love, we kind of expect it with God, but the neighbour bit seems a bit unfair. Love your neighbour as much as yourself is kind of demanding. But that's the radical side to being a Christian that should make us completely different to anyone else. When we have needs we sort them out – if we are hungry, we eat; lonely, we find a friend; unhappy, we look out for something to pick us up. When Jesus tells us to love our neighbour as we love ourselves, he's encouraging us to look out for other people's needs as well as our own.

Luke 10:30-33 – *'A man was going down from Jerusalem to Jericho, when he fell into the hands of robbers. They stripped him of his clothes, beat him and went away leaving him half dead. A priest happened to be going down the same road, and when he saw the man, he passed by on the other side. So too, a Levite, when he came to the place and saw him, passed by on the other side. But a Samaritan, as he travelled, came where the man was; and when he saw him took pity on him.'*

The Samaritan bandaged his wounds, took him to an inn and saw to his every need. He demonstrated love when the so-called religious people ignored the man, leaving him for dead. As Christians we must be sure to show love and not be religious with words only. Whether it be helping a person involved in a road accident, giving money to the starving in distant lands, or being a friend to someone being bullied, make sure you act rather than ignore the need and don't be religious with words only!

Romans 14:19-21 – *'Let us therefore make every effort to do what leads to peace and mutual edification. Do not destroy the work of God for the sake of food. All food is clean, but it is wrong for a man to eat something that causes someone else to stumble. It is better not to eat meat or drink wine or to do anything else that will cause your brother or sister to fall'*

This is not really about meat eaters versus vegetarians, about Gentiles eating food Jews did not eat. Paul instructs the Gentile believers to do nothing that will offend or insult the Jewish believers. The same principle applies to us, we should never say or do anything that will offend or hurt other people. When you spot a person's need, be sensitive in how you deal with them; don't put them down or give offence like Hannah did, but be relevant and approachable, friendly and loving. Make sure there is nothing which might prevent others from coming to you for help!

Listening point

The Bible contains some amazing verses. Could you list some? Well, in case your list doesn't include this one, think about adding it – 'To all who received him, to those who believed in his name, he gave the right to become children of God' (John 1:12). In other words, if you believe in Jesus, follow him and trust him for your life here on earth and then in heaven – it means you are his child! Being a child of God is kind of unbelievable because it means God makes his home within us. That means that inside of us is the one who stretched out his hands and made the universe, the one who stretched out his hands and hung on a cross, and the one who longs to stretch out his hands and touch the hurting needs of every person you will meet or walk past today.

I think the greatest need of people today is that they need to be *loved*. How many people do you know who don't have loving parents or real mates? How many people do you know who feel really low about life and as if they don't matter? How many people do you know who feel like real failures, feel that they have never got anything right and most likely never will? The answer will most likely be, 'too many'. Our big wide world is very demanding and when people fail it can be very unloving! Most people are broken and hurting and in every case Jesus wants to reach out and help them. How does he do it?

An Old testament prophet describes how he heard the voice of the Lord saying, 'Whom shall I send? And who will go for us?' (Isaiah 6:8). God usually restricts himself to working through his people. But who are his people? His children. So who are his children? You and me!

Isaiah never forgot what happened next. I said, 'Here am I. Send me!' He said. 'Go … ' (Isaiah 6:8–9).

Are we willing to go and be Jesus to those people we bump into every day, who are hurting and have great needs? To show Jesus and act as he did (2 Corinthians 5:20), to reach out and touch the pain of the broken and needy? Are we willing to allow Jesus within us to stretch out his hands of love and to heal? Isn't that what he told us to do as his children? He told his disciples, 'All authority in heaven and on earth has been given to me. Therefore go … ' (Matthew 28:18–19). In truth we have only two choices: we can either ignore God's voice just as the priest and Levite ignored the dying man on the roadside, or we can go and be obedient, which results in our helping to change our world. As his children, we have all the authority Jesus has, and the fullness of God living within us. The Bible says, 'I can do everything through him who gives me strength' (Philippians 4:13).

At the very start of Jesus' ministry he stood in the synagogue with Jewish worshippers listening to his every word. He unrolled the scroll of Isaiah and read:

> *The Spirit of the Lord is on me,*
> *because he has anointed me*
> *to preach good news to the poor.*
> *He has sent me to proclaim freedom*
> *for the prisoners*
> *and recovery of sight for the blind,*
> *to release the oppressed,*
> *to proclaim the year of the Lord's favour*
> (Luke 4: 18–19).

Then with every eye upon him, the suspense building, he looked at his audience and said, 'Today this scripture is fulfilled in your hearing' (Luke 4:21). In other words, 'I am the one whom Isaiah wrote about, I am the Christ'. His words bounce off the ceiling, leaving the audience in anger and disbelief.

Other people feel differently. To a woman caught in adultery Jesus brought freedom, to the sick he offered healing, to the chief priest he opens the door of heaven, to a prostitute he gave friendship, and he raised his dead friend back to life. Jesus publicly acknowledged a social outcast, and to a common thief on a cross he gave eternal life. Wherever he went, whoever he talked with, he offered *good news*, *freedom*, and *healing*. He was indeed the one Isaiah talked about and he lives in you!

Remember, the one who brought good news, freedom, and healing is longing to touch and change the lives of the needy people you meet today, and this may include friends, family, and other people in your life. Let's allow him to, and let's be open and available to say, 'Here I am, send me!'

Radical Action Guide

1. At the start of every day, ask God to show you at least one person who is in need and whom you can help through Christ who strengthens you.
2. Look out for people in your life – watch how they behave and look. Figure out if they have any needs and then consider how you can help them.
3. Don't ignore distant needs such as famines; consider ways of raising the profile of the disasters that people don't know or don't care about. Work out a way to raise funds to help.
4. Be sensitive to people who have obvious needs, don't rush in like a bulldozer (Hannah), but don't sit back and never help.
5. To every person you ever meet be kind, warm, encouraging, and approachable. Your simple acceptance of a person could just be the spark somebody needs to begin recovery.

the **Needy** Loving as yourself

Take a moment...

...to look at this diagram; think for a moment about the 3 areas. Then try and identify people in your life who are in need and how you can help them with whatever that need is. Remember you can do all things through Christ who strengthens you (Phil 4:13)

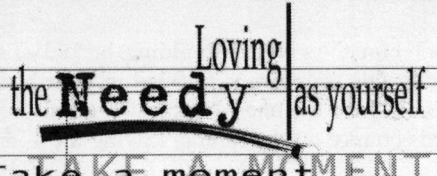

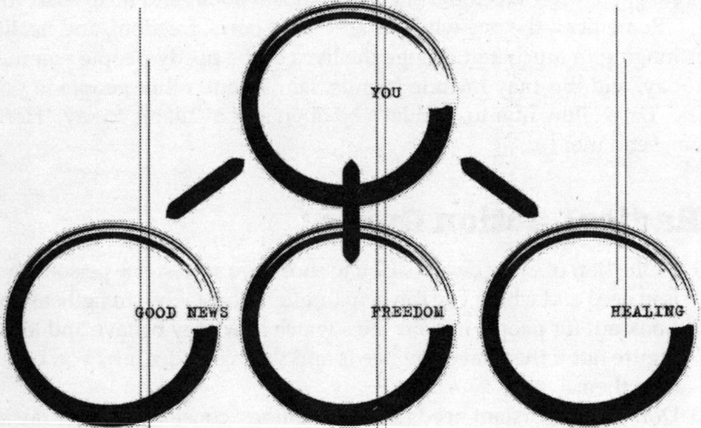

YOU

GOOD NEWS — FREEDOM — HEALING

Who	How	Who	How	Who	How

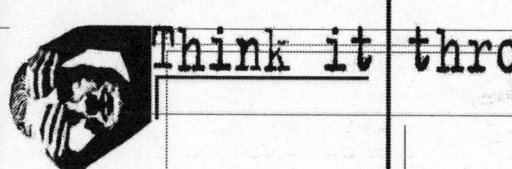
Think it through...

General Notes...

Encouraged by...

discouraged by...

I need to Change...

EVALUATE
✓ Get it RIGHT!

Obedience

The big issue

'Didn't I tell you what I would do if you ever disobeyed me?' Fourteen-year-old Gerry ran for the door, with his father in hot pursuit. 'Dad, I didn't mean to ... ' Smack. The back of his father's hand swept across Gerry's face, instantly drawing blood from his nose. The force of the blow knocked Gerry to the floor. His father now towered over him.

'I told you to bring the bottle to me, *didn't I?!*' he yelled at the top of his voice.

The terrified boy began to cry, 'Dad, I dropped it, it was an accident'. His tears were flowing fast and blending with the blood pouring from his nose.

'*You dropped it*', whispered his father. Then he bent down and grabbed Gerry's T-shirt, ripping it at the neck. 'You didn't drop it you liar. You drank it; be a man, admit it!' With that, he lifted his hand above his head, clenching his fist so the knuckles turned white.

Gerry, knowing what was coming, began pleading, 'Please Dad, please ... I didn't drink it, I prom ... ' The force of the punch knocked Gerry senseless. The fourteen-year-old lay deathly still, with no sign of life except when his lungs gasped for air. This was the fourth time Gerry's nose had been broken, and one of his teeth lay on the floor. His father stood up, headed for the sideboard, and poured himself a drink.

Talking point

Gerry's father was an alcoholic. As a child Gerry had watched his mother suffer both physically and emotionally, and now as a teenager he was getting the same treatment. On this occasion, Gerry had neither drunk the alcohol nor smashed the bottle – he had hidden it in the hope of protecting the family from more acts of drunken violence. The plan had failed and Gerry was severely punished for it.

- Did Gerry do the right thing in disobeying his father?
- What would you have done if you had been Gerry?
- In what circumstances do you think it right to disobey someone?
- Do you find being told what to do easy?
- What things do you most hate being told to do?
- Why is obedience generally good for us?
- When can obedience be bad for us?
- Have you ever been told to do something and disobeyed, resulting either in injury or other negative outcome?

Bible point

God shows us what he expects of us.
'He has showed you, O people, what is good. And what does the Lord require of you? To act justly and to love mercy and to walk humbly with your God' Micah 6:8.

Obedience leads to success.
'Do not let this Book of the Law depart from your mouth; meditate on it day and night, so that you may be careful to do everything written in it. Then you will be prosperous and successful' Joshua 1:8.

Fullness of life is given to those who obey.
'Well done, good and faithful servant! You have been faithful with a few things; I will put you in charge of many things. Come and share your master's happiness!' Matthew 25:21.

Listening point

The vast majority of people in this world know that their parents love them to pieces,[1] but there are some parents who are not the best example of love, and some of them don't even know what love is. Gerry's father was one of these, so caught up in his own world, his own pain and addiction, that he could not see the pain and abuse he was inflicting on his own son. One thing is certain: Gerry has a heavenly Father, just like you and I have, who just longs to heap as much love as possible on us. Unlike human parents, God is neither short of love nor caught up in his own pain. Quite the opposite – he wants to take our pain and fill us with love over and over again. For Gerry's father, authority meant slavery – 'do this or else!', whereas God the Father uses his authority in love. When God asks us to be obedient he doesn't get a kick out of his power over us, he does it because whatever he's asking us to do is what is best for us, what is safe and good for us. There won't be any beating or shouting if we get it wrong, there won't be anger or rejection when we fail or disobey, just more and more love.

In the Bible we find God's commands for his people, and what he expects of them. Sometimes it all seems a bit much, sometimes we are just too tired, and sometimes it doesn't seem fair. But there is not one rule in the Bible that wasn't put there to help us or protect us. The Ten Commandments were given out of love. The Sermon on the Mount was given out of love. If you want to know how to do well in life, how to get on with people, how to lead a healthy and emotionally balanced life, just turn the pages of your Bible and it's all there. You will find instruction after instruction on how to follow God and be a far better person for it.

If we are serious about following Jesus and living as a child of God, then there is a price to be paid. It's not easy to be a Christian, it's not easy to do everything the Bible says, but God's Holy Spirit helps you. Jesus said to His disciples (and to us), 'If you love me, you will obey what I command. And I will ask the Father, and he will give you another Counsellor to be with you for ever – the Spirit of truth. The world cannot accept him, because it neither sees him nor knows him. But you know him, for he lives with you and will be in you' (John 14:15-17). Yes, God promised to come himself to live within you (1 Corinthians 6:19), to help and guide you and to come alongside you when you are in need. Sometimes, when it's tough, we may well feel alone, but the fact is, God is with us every step of the way and ready to help us out during moments of temptation. Thousands of years ago God made a promise to all who follow him, and that promise is for you today – He said that he 'will never leave you nor forsake you' (Deuteronomy 31:6).

Although God has expectations of us, he helps us to learn from our mistakes when we fail. The author of the letter to Hebrew Christians says that we should expect God to discipline us when we fail. For if we aren't disciplined we are not his children (Hebrews 12:5–13). But God doesn't discipline us like Gerry's father, he doesn't dock our salary or take away the most amazing girl or boyfriend we've ever had. No, he speaks to us in a way that only God can, and when we eventually realise what he's saying, we begin to learn from our mistakes.

Time and time again, the Bible tells us to obey earthly authority figures such as the government, parents or teachers. It is crucial that we should show respect and obedience to people older and wiser than we are (more on that in the chapter on Parents), not to do that is disobey God! But there are, and will be, times in your life when you are asked to do something that is questionable. For Christians in various parts of the world, believing in Jesus is illegal. Every time they worship, they break the law. Should they obey the law and renounce their faith? No, at a time like that, the Bible teaches us to 'obey God rather than human beings' (Acts 5:29). Occasionally, an authority figure like a teacher or youth leader may ask you to compromise yourself by doing something wrong. It could be as small as to sit in an over-crowded car with no seats or safety belts available. To do it is illegal and again, at times like that, you have every right to say no and disobey. Earthly authority is there to protect and preserve people but as we have already discovered with Gerry's father, occasionally that authority is blatantly abused. The point being made is quite simple – when your heavenly Father asks you to do something, however strange it might be, it will never be to hurt you – it will only out of love. Unless you live in a country where religious freedom is restricted, he is unlikely to ask you to break the law and his commands are for the good of everyone. When we know God is asking us to do something, we should do it without a second thought. Remember though, he will never ask you to do something that goes against Scripture, and the best way to find out what he wants you to do is by reading his commands for you in the Bible. When someone asks us to do something, we should immediately weigh it in the light of our faith. 'Does what I'm being asked to do in anyway contradict what God asks of me through the Bible?' The answer to that will be almost always 'No'.

Once Jesus was asked what is the greatest commandment. He replied '"Love the Lord your God with all your heart and with all your soul and with all your mind and with all your strength." The second is this: "Love your neighbour as yourself"' (Mark 12:30–31). In that reply can be found the very heart of our faith. If you want to live for Jesus, then love him, and love others. If you truly love him, then you will do what he asks you to by the help of his Spirit, and day by day you will slowly change to be more and more like him.

Radical Action Guide

If you really want to be the best that you can be for God, to love him and live the life he's asked of you, then follow these 3 simple steps:

1. Read his instructions.
2. Discover what they actually mean.
3. Apply them to your life by doing what they say.

Please note that in no case is it acceptable or legal for a parent or anyone else to beat a child (as in Gerry's case). If you or anyone you know has been, or is being beaten, then there are caring people who would like to help you bring the violence to an end. You can speak to them in private and in confidence from any telephone, free of charge, at Child Line. If you feel you are in immediate danger phone the police on 999, or visit a local police station. Don't ever feel ashamed of phoning, for you have done nothing wrong. There are various other people you could visit such as a teacher, social services, your local doctor, church minister or youth leader.

---

[1] See the chapter on parents

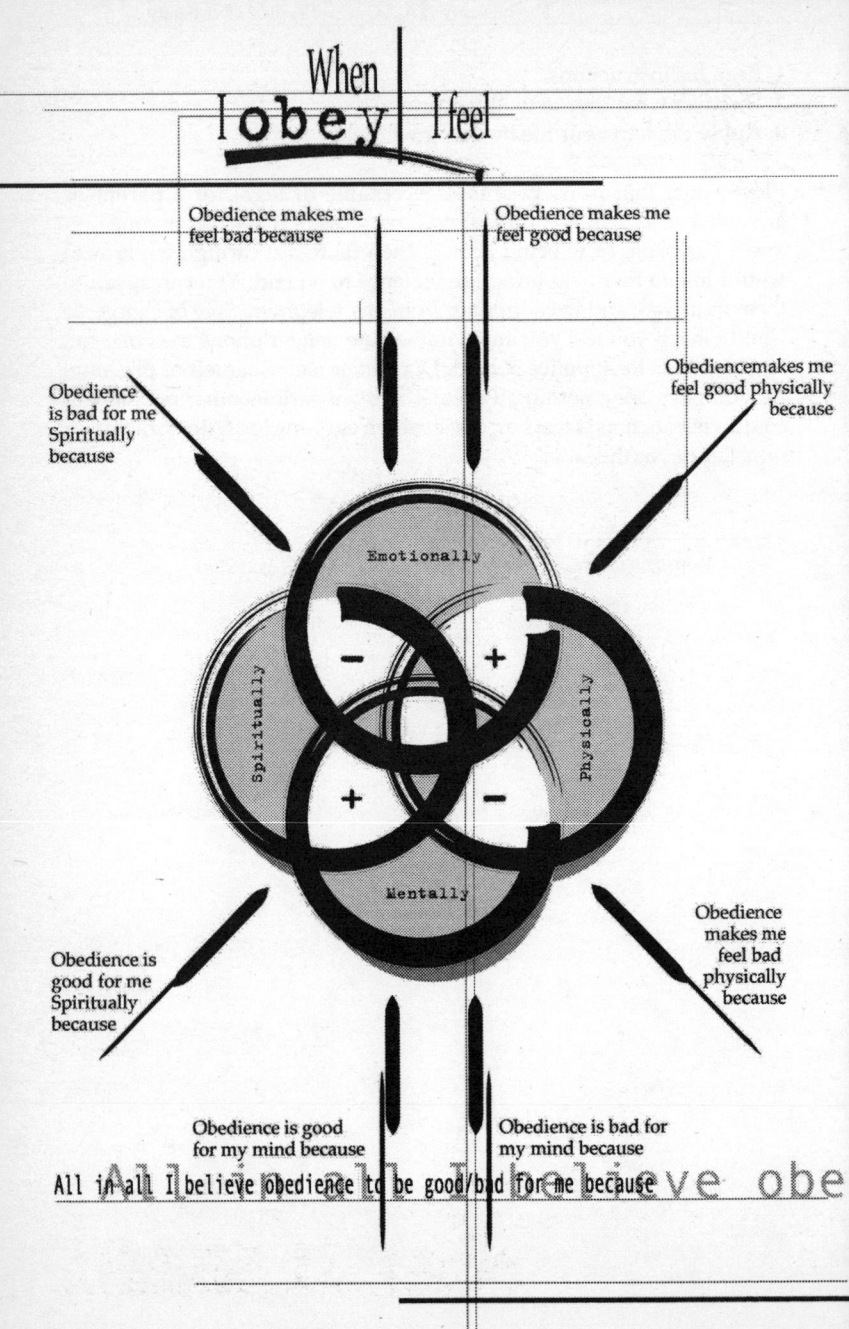

Think it through...

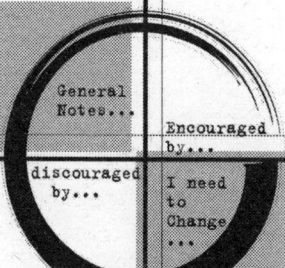

General Notes...

Encouraged by...

discouraged by...

I need to Change ...

EVALUATE

✓ Get it RIGHT!

Parents

The big issue

'No!' Josh's mother shouted across the hall. Josh screamed back, 'I don't care what you say, I'm going!' His mother raised her voice retaliating, 'You're not!' and she took a few steps forward. 'I am and there is not a thing you can do to stop me.' With that Josh slammed the bedroom door shut. Josh's mother, feeling the blast of air from the door, was now ready and hungry for a fight. 'You listen here ... ' She was stopped in mid-flow, only to find her son had locked the door. The temperature gauge rose a few more degrees and in a low bass tone, she spat out a warning message. 'Open this door now.' She paused, waiting for a response. Moments went by but nothing happened.

'Joshua, you open this door NOW!! One thing is for sure you are not going out to see your mates and you will not be going out for the next two weeks ... ' As if a torpedo had been launched through the keyhole, a hundred decibel roar boomed through her body. She stopped speaking in mid flow with her mouth wide open and her face was a picture of terror. The building vibrated, no amount of screaming or banging on the door could possibly be heard above the deadly music coming from the room, and in defeat she hastily retreated, to phone his father. One hour later when the music had faded, and the noise had stopped ringing in his mother's ears, she found Josh's bedroom door wide open – he had long since gone to see his friends. 'You wait till your father gets home, Joshua!' threatened his mother to an empty lifeless bedroom.

Talking point

- Is your home ever like Josh's home? In what way?
- Josh was frustrated with his mother for not letting him go out with his friends. How do you deal with your frustrations?

- Do you think Josh was right to show his frustrations like that towards his mum? If not, how should he have acted?
- Do you think parents should have the final say?
- What is the worst and most unfair thing your mum or dad have ever told you to do?
- Can you remember a time when your mum or dad asked you to do something that you didn't want to do, but now looking back, you can see the wisdom of it?
- What are some of the things you vow never to do to your kids that your parents have done to you?
- What are some of the really good things your parents have done to you that you would like to copy if you had kids of your own?
- Do you think being a parent is easy?

Bible point

Exodus 20:12 – *'Honour your father and your mother, so that you may live long in the land the Lord your God is giving you'*
God rates being good, courteous, obedient and respectful to your parents so important that He included it as one of His basic ten commandments. So strong is God's desire for you to obey this command that there is the promise attached of a good future for you if you do obey it. Every time we honour our parents, we also honour our God. That in itself should be a reason for holding our tongues at the hottest and most tense of moments when one of our parents has just done the most irritating and embarrassing thing to us.

Ephesians 6:1 – *'Children obey your parents ... '*
Isn't that the same as 'honour your parents?' Actually, no, to honour as we have already seen is to respect and be polite, whereas to obey is to do as you are told. Josh and almost every teenager who ever lived has struggled with obeying an insensitive, prehistoric parent who can't remember being younger than 45 (even if they haven't reached 45). God expects you to do what you are told unless a parent's instructions are either illegal or cause you to disobey Him. Tough one!

Proverbs 1:8 – *'Listen my son, to your father's instruction and do not forsake your mother's teaching'*

What on earth is all that about? Well, in truth, we mainly learn by being shown rather than being told. Many of the values you have and things you view as important have been handed down by your parents, more or less through their actions and attitudes. It may come as a surprise to you, but your mum and dad have lived life, they have experienced pain as well as success. They have a lot of wisdom to pass on. It may at times seem as though it's tightly locked in their heads but if you give them more than 30 seconds of your time you might be surprised to find out they have a lot of amazing things to tell you about – you may even be surprised to find it's actually helpful! Give it a go …

Ephesians 6:4 – *'Fathers, do not exasperate your children; instead, bring them up in the training and instruction of the Lord'*

Home should be a place of security and comfort, a place where you can be you. Sure, it's also a place where you are disciplined and told off when you are wrong, but it's never meant to be anything other than a fortress of love and safety. Sometimes parents get it wrong, sometimes parents act in haste, but if you don't feel safe because of the actions of one or both of your parents, then your home is not how God planned it to be for you.[1]

Listening point

Could there be anything more frustrating, more irritating, more annoying than a parent? How is it they live with their heads buried in the sand, totally unaware of reality – completely unaware of what life for you as a teenager can be like. Instead of being understanding, they get cross, say the exact opposite to what you need to hear, or tell you to stop being stupid and act your age or grow up or something just as offensive! Is that how it is for you?

Well, from another point of view, it's not that easy being a parent either. Most parents have the stress of work, paying the bills, running the house and looking after you and any brothers or sisters you may have. If you're from a one parent family, or if one of your parents is away a lot, then it's even harder. Raising a child to be a teenager ready for whatever life has to throw at them is probably the hardest job in the world. Landing a 747 without any wheels is easier than that; and you know, nobody teaches or trains parents – they don't go to school and receive qualifications and degrees in how to raise kids. In other words, most parents don't actually know what they are doing and are learning as they go along. Sure, they are going to make mistakes, some mistakes are going to be terrible! So terrible you just want to scream and burn the house down, but rather than curse them, rather than make life hell because they have upset you, take a moment to try and see things from their side of the fence. When you're seeing things from their point of view, you may still think they have acted wrongly or made an unfair decision, and it could well be that they have. But, take your time, turn the boiler of your emotions down and at a later date tell them in a mature and non-accusing manner that you struggled to see their point and would like them to explain it to you.

Most important of all, you need to realize that when a parent is frothing at the mouth and bright red in the face over something you have done or said or asked them, they still love you. Yep, it's the weirdest way of expressing love, but parents are occasionally frightened. They love you to bits, since you were born they have looked after you, made decisions, and worried about you. They are worried that if they don't scream at you, or punish you then you might grow up to be a psychopathic murderer, or if they don't stop you from going out to see your friends then something awful may happen like your being abducted by aliens. Parents are people and they have their reasons. It's just trying to see and understand those reasons that can be tough. But it can be tough for them to see your side as well. If you're a person who likes to slam doors, curse, shout, scream, or run off after a discussion or completely ignore what they told you to do, then you've got to realize your actions don't make a great deal of rational sense either!

Well, here is the tough part: God wants us to do what our parents say – he wants us to respect them and obey them. (Exodus 20:12, Ephesians 6:1) They are the ones who are responsible for you. They are also the ones who are doing everything that they believe to be best for you. You might not always agree with that – staying out all night may not be a problem in your eyes, but don't count on your mother or father seeing it that way. Do what's right when you just want to explode with frustration when you have made plans with your friends, and your parents are the only ones to say no, while all the other mums or dads have said yes. Accept the decision, don't react – take time to chew it over and if you still don't agree, ask them to explain it again. But even if you don't like it the second time round, bite your tongue and step back.

The hardest thing of all can be when one or both of your parents doesn't believe in God, or doesn't care about him in any real way. As Christians, nearly everything we do, think and act on is related to our faith and belief, and if they don't share those views, or don't support you in them – or even worse, think your crazy, then it can be painful! But your Heavenly Father sees the situation, He understands what you're dealing with and your support can be found in him. You have two advantages over your parents here, one is the Holy Spirit living in you and the other is prayer. Both change lives – your life and theirs!

If you want to do what's right at home, then it's going to take guts and plenty of humble pie, because obedience and respect don't come naturally to anyone. Yet that's what it takes to make things work. When things do fail, and you find you've smashed a plate in anger for having to do the dishes 4 nights in a row, or you let slip a few thoughts you wish you had kept to yourself, then make sure you sort it out and always say sorry. The Bible says, 'Do not let the sun go down while you are still angry'. (Ephesians 4:26) In other words, deal with it before the day ends and don't let it go on to spoil another day. Remember more than anything else: your parents love you. They may be terrible at showing it, but they do![2] And if they aren't too hot at expressing their love, then help them out by showing yours. Being a parent and being a son or daughter is a partnership – it takes two to make it work! Therefore help to make it work and enjoy it!

Radical Action Guide

Help your parents to be the best that they can be by:
1. Loving them.
2. Supporting them.
3. Helping them out.
4. Obeying them.
5. Listening to them.
6. Talking to them.
7. Responding calmly and patiently to problems.
8. Giving instead of taking.
9. Being sensitive to what's happening in their lives as well as yours.
10. Praying for them.

---

1 See boxed note at the end of listening point, in the chapter on Obedience.

2 If you really feel one or both of your parents don't love you, that can be more painful than anything else in the world. You need to talk with someone about that. Take a look at the listening point in the Obedience chapter. But more importantly go and talk to a friend, church minister or your youth worker – tell them how you feel and why you feel that way. You deserve to be loved, it's every child's right and by talking with someone it may help you to discover a side to one or both of your parents you never thought was there.

Being a parent

My Parents raised me (with)...

	tick			tick
Love			No love	
Discipline			No discipline	
Care			No care	
Guidelines			No guidelines	
Healthily			Unhealthily	
Balance			No balance	
Kindness			No kindness	
Respect			No respect	
Prayer			No prayer	
What's best for me			No interest in me	

Above

What do your answers tell you about how your parents raised you?

What do your answers tell you about how you sometimes act towards your parents?

Is there anything or any attitude you may have that you need to change towards your parents?

Below

How similar are your answers to how your parents raised you?

Do your answers in anyway alter your opinion towards how your parents raised you?

If I were a Parent I ...

	tick			tick
Would allow my child to do anything he or she wanted to			Would not allow my child to do anything he or she wanted to	
Would allow my child to eat or drink anything he or she wanted to			Would not allow my child to eat or drink anything he or she wanted to	
Would allow my child to speak to me any way he or she wanted to			Would not allow my child to speak to me any way he or she wanted to	
Would allow my child to have and spend as much money as he or she wanted to			Would not allow my child to have and spend as much money as he or she wanted to	
Would allow my child to dress / see whoever he or she wanted to			Would not allow my child to dress / see whoever he or she wanted to	

Think it through...

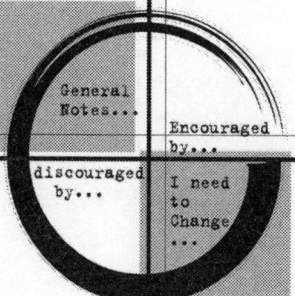

General Notes...   Encouraged by...

discouraged by...   I need to Change...

EVALUATE

✓ Get it RIGHT!

Quiet Time

The big issue

Jude had been given a book about prayer by her youth worker. She had admitted in a meeting that she didn't find prayer very easy and she never really had much time. The book told her that if she was a believer, then prayer was essential and she should spend at least 30 minutes a day in prayer. The right time for prayer wasn't last thing at night but first thing in the morning before the rest of the house stirred. For Jude that meant half-past five, since she had a younger brother who got out of bed at six o'clock sharp. The first morning, with book in hand, Jude was there at 5:30. Since she didn't actually know what to say or do, she just read her book. Throughout that day Jude was exhausted. She didn't usually get out of bed until eight o'clock and her early start had come as a real sacrifice and shock. The next morning she didn't manage 5:30 but was on her knees by 5:45 – blurry-eyed and with virtually no brain power she muttered a few words before drifting into a trance for the next ten minutes. The next day Jude slept through till 5:55 and in the remaining five minutes, more or less managed to say, 'Dear Lord, good morning … please bless … (yawn) … today'.

The following morning Jude didn't even manage to wake up until half-past seven. She spent the entire day feeling tired and whacked after her three early morning starts – guilty too for not making it work. The following week Jude gave the book back to the leader and told him, 'Thanks, but this praying thing is not for me, I'm just no good at it!'

Talking point

- ◆ Have you ever felt like Jude, when prayer is a struggle and you feel guilty?
- ◆ Why do you think Jude failed?
- ◆ Do you think we should feel guilty if we find both praying and

finding time to pray difficult?

- What is prayer?
- What is having a quiet time?
- Have you ever prayed for something or someone and what you prayed for happened?
- What do you find hardest about having a quiet time?
- What is the best thing for you in having a quiet time?

Bible point

God speaks to us in the quiet times.
'The Lord said, "Go out and stand on the mountain in the presence of the Lord, for the Lord is about to pass by". Then a great and powerful wind tore the mountains apart and shattered the rocks before the Lord, but the Lord was not in the wind. After the wind there was an earthquake, but the Lord was not in the earthquake. After the earthquake came a fire, but the Lord was not in the fire. And after the fire came a gentle whisper. When Elijah heard it, he pulled his cloak over his face and went out and stood at the mouth of the cave. Then a voice said to him, "What are you doing here, Elijah?"' 1 Kings 19:11-13.

God shows us how to pray.
'This then is how you should pray: "Our Father in heaven, hallowed be your name, your kingdom come, your will be done on earth as it is in heaven. Give us today our daily bread ... And lead us not into temptation, but deliver us from the evil one" Matthew 6:9-13.

God reveals his plans and desires for us in the Bible.
'Do not let this Book of the Law depart from your mouth; meditate on it day and night, so that you may be careful to do everything written in it. Then you will be prosperous and successful' Joshua 1:8.

Listening point

If your minister ever wanted to put his congregation on a guilt trip, all he would need to do would be to preach about the importance of Christians praying and reading their Bibles each day. The congregation would immediately feel guilty because most Christians are terrible at finding time to pray and read their Bibles, and when they do, they sometimes don't understand what they are reading, or know what to pray – or spend the entire time with a glazed expression on their faces or even worse, fall asleep. Having a quiet time is neither natural nor easy; don't let someone more 'spiritual' than you let you think otherwise. So if you struggle with prayer and reading your Bible, join the club most believers belong to.

However, that doesn't mean we should be apathetic and not bother. The whole thing about being a Christian is that we have a relationship with God. If you have a relationship with someone, two things are important: one is communication and the other is interest. If you don't talk or show any interest, it isn't a great relationship and this is true for our relationship with God. But before you start to feel guilty – don't! The last thing God wants of us is to feel guilty about being 'spiritual' failures. Paul tells us, to be like that is a load of rubbish – (Philippians 3: 1-11). God knows what we are like – he still loves us and will keep on loving us. That will never change; he doesn't want us to become depressed and miserable, rather, he wants us to come to him because of his love and not because of a sense of guilt.

Luke 5:16 tells us a small but remarkable fact about Jesus. It says, that he 'often withdrew to lonely places and prayed'. Jesus escaped from the world to be alone with his Father, to spend quality time talking and listening! That doesn't sound too difficult does it? It even sounds kind of attractive …

A man who lived a thousand or so years before Jesus described what it means to be a godly person '..their delight is in the law of the Lord, and on his law they meditate day and night' (Psalm 1:2). The law means God's book (the Bible). The psalmist delighted to read it because it was good, helpful, encouraging, full of truths about God, and how to live his way. If we want our soul to be fed and to grow, then we need to be like this and delight in God's word. We might not always understand it, but we can start with the Psalms and the New Testament because there's plenty there to get us going.

One important instruction for prayer is, 'Be still and know that I am God' (Psalm 46:10). Basically, God is saying to us, 'Stop rushing around, trying to do this, that, and the other. Stop talking and just be quiet before me, then you will know who I really am. I am God!' I don't know about you, but I can't stay still for very long before I either get an itch to do something, or I feel guilty for being lazy. Well here it is, we are told to do nothing, and to enjoy doing nothing. But it's doing nothing in God's presence that counts, and your spirit will encounter God in an amazing way, just like Elijah did on the mountain. Elijah didn't find God in all the commotion or noise but in the silence.

When do *you* pray? The psalmist tells us that he would get up to pray before the day had begun. There is a lot of wisdom in that, because then we give ourselves and our day over to God afresh! But you may think, 'He was probably a morning person!' And it's certainly true that not everyone is an early riser whose brain can function beyond seeing to their primary physical needs (toilet, breakfast …). For some, like Jude, mornings are just not the best time! Try, though, to do what Jesus did, and at some point in the day find a quiet place on your own to be with God. Read some of God's word, take time to tell him how you feel, how much you love Him, what you or others need help over, and then be quiet just to listen. Whether you give ten minutes or as much as an hour is up to you. Praying can be like exercise: start slowly and in time it gets easier and you can do more. But most of all be assured that what matters to God is not what you say or do, or how long you give, but the simple fact that the child whom he adores has come to be with him.

Radical Action Guide

Suggested guidelines for your quiet time:

1. Find a quiet place.
2. Take time to praise God (e.g. Psalm 8).
3. Take time to say thank you for all the things he has done for you or others. (e.g. Psalm 107:1-3).
4. Take time to say sorry for the times you have failed him or others (e.g. 1 John 1:9).
5. Take time to pray for other people and their needs (e.g. Romans 15:30).
6. Take time to ask God for things you need (e.g. Matthew 7:7–8).
7. Take time to reflect on God and his word (e.g. Joshua 1:8).
8. Take time to be quiet and listen (e.g. 1 Samuel 3:9).

the Quiet Time Pyramid

Place a tick next to the step that best describes your quiet times. Then take one word from the list below (or you can add your own) that expresses how you feel and place it in the box you identified.

I find prayer very easy, natural and always hear God speak

I find prayer exciting and always learn or hear something from God

Most of the time I pray I benefit from it and sometimes I hear from God

Prayer is not that easy for me, occassionally I really feel touched by God

Prayer is hard work and more often than not I don't feel that God has spoken to me

Prayer is constant and most the time I leave disappointed

I find prayer dull and boring, I don't understand my Bible and God never speaks to me

I don't think God has ever answered my prayers and it feels a waste of time

I hardly ever pray and when ever I do, I wish that I hadn't

I never pray or read my Bible, I know I should but I don't instead I just feel guilty

HAppy, Bored, Ecstatic, Dull, Inspired, Uninspired, Anointed, Depressed, Fruitful, Time wasting, Enthusiastic, Hard, Encouraged, Apathetic, Blessed, Unhappy, Impressed, Sad, Touched, Disappointed, Cool, Have given up

1. From your own description and added word is your prayer life, healthy, growing, slipping or at rock bottom?
2. Do you see room for improvement?

Think it through...

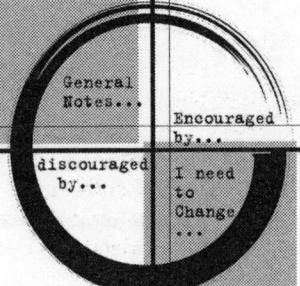

General Notes...
Encouraged by...
discouraged by...
I need to Change...

EVALUATE

✓ Get it RIGHT!

Relationships

The big issue

Tammy opened the letter. 'Why ever should Nicky write to me?' she asked out loud. Since Nicky lived just two blocks away and they saw each other every day, it seemed strange to get a letter. The letter started off pleasantly enough. Nicky described how much Tammy had meant as a friend for the last three years. That was fine – until she reached the part that said, ' I'm writing this because, however special you may be to me, I know our friendship has been wrong from the start. I am a Christian and I have always wanted to believe that the fact that you are not should not be an issue. But it is, and I know that now. The Bible says, 'Don't mix with unbelievers'. The fact that you are my friend means I am sinning. However sad this may be for both of us, this letter must be the end'. At first Tammy was amused, thinking Nicky was joking, but there was an edge to the letter that was far more serious, cruel and final rather than funny. 'Yeah, she is serious,' thought Tammy. They had been best friends for such a long time – Nicky was the only real friend Tammy had ever had. She didn't understand what Nicky meant by 'sinning'. What kind of God would demand this she wondered.

Talking point

- ◆ Do you think Nicky was or was not right as a Christian to end her close friendship with Tammy, explain your reasons.
- ◆ How would you have felt if you had been Tammy?
- ◆ Do you think we should have strict rules to guide our relationships?
- ◆ Should the standards for our relationships with non-Christian friends be different from those we apply with Christian friends?

- If your answer to either of the previous two questions is 'yes,' then what kind of rules would you have?

Rules for relationships with non-Christians	Rules for relationships with Christians
1.	
2.	
3.	
4.	
5.	

- Do you think it's OK to have a really close friendship with just one person (your best friend) or is that too cliquey and unfair to others?

- Do you think it is actually possible for your best friend or the friend you spend most time with to be of the opposite sex and for you not to be sexually attracted at all to them? How? (answer honestly)

Bible point

1 Samuel 20:42 – *'Jonathan said to David, "Go in peace, for we have sworn friendship with each other in the name of the Lord"'*
Jonathan and David were the very best of friends, so much so that they were prepared to risk their lives for each other. Jonathan loved his friend so much that when his father, King Saul, wanted to kill David, Jonathan did everything to protect his friend even when it meant falling out of his father's favour. Surely the greatest mark of any friendship is that of loyalty and commitment. However rare it may be, such a relationship is worth finding and keeping.

2 Corinthians 6:14 – *'Do not be yoked together with unbelievers. For what do righteousness and wickedness have in common? Or what fellowship can light have with darkness?'*
When Paul wrote this part of Corinthians he wasn't directly thinking of Christians having friendships with unbelievers. He was referring to the false prophets and teachers who were trying to mix with the new church and pollute it. His point, though, can apply to our non-Christian friends. Do they in any way weaken your faith, tempt you or encourage you to do things that you know are not right and that God would not be

pleased with? If they do then the friendship is not good for you and your light is being dimmed by the surrounding darkness. Don't put yourself in a situation where you know for sure that your faith and belief could be damaged.

Proverbs 17:17 – *'A friend loves at all times, and kinsfolk are born to share adversity'*
Most of our friendships aren't exactly deep. You usually don't know too much about the person you sit next to in class or work alongside in your job. Sure, you share a laugh with them, or maybe even admit to them if things in your life are not going well, but beyond that, are you close? Few of our relationships with people are so close that you know they will do anything they can to help you in trouble, or will show real interest in a part of your life which most people would find boring. Do you have any friends as close as that? If you do, then they are worth more to you than any amount of money!

Listening point

Nobody likes being told what to do, but being told who you can or cannot have as a friend is outrageous. It's not unheard of for a parent, teacher or youth leader to tell you your mate is not exactly a saint and they don't think you should hang around with them! It kind of jars on you when they say, 'we've noticed a difference in you and it's not for the better!' Maybe someone has said that to you about one of your friends, or even worse, maybe one of your friend's parents has said that about you!

The greatest moment in your life so far, the saddest moment you have encountered, the time you laughed so much you nearly wet yourself, or your most sobering experience almost certainly involved other people. We are created to be social beings. We actually need others; some people don't think so, but it's a fact! Nothing can make you more angry, disgust you so much or make you so unbelievably happy as another person! We need relationships. They are essential: whether they are close and intense with a best friend or boy/girlfriend, or a deep and significant bond with a parent or family member, or the need for company with your mates. They may only be casual relationships – it could be a partner in gym class that you only ever see for 30 minutes a week, or the baker you buy your sandwiches from, or even the bloke who hangs around the centre of town selling the 'Big Issue'. If you connect in any way with anyone then you have a relationship and that relationship, however big or small, however often or seldom it enters your mind, is important to your life.

Why is it that we may not want to see a film for the fifth time on TV, but when someone who's never seen it before sits down to watch it with us, our level of pleasure rises from the pits of boredom to the same feelings we had the very first time we watched it? Why is it we hate walking in the rain, but don't even notice it when someone walks and talks with us? And why is it that when we are really low or when we have some great news, we look for someone to share it with? Without relationships, we are mentally, physically, socially, and even spiritually incomplete people. We were created to interact, to be encouraged by another person's smile, comforted by a touch, stimulated by a conversation, inspired by the actions of others, relaxed by the sharing of jokes and laughter, and delighting in the physical presence and company of another. People matter to us whether you know it or not!

Any relationship can have both good and bad influences. When your parents grill you about who your friends are, where you go, what you do, it's because they know that although you may well be an incredibly positive influence on others, you yourself may still be open to being influenced by them into different thoughts and actions. Could there be anything more worrying to a parent than someone your age giving you even a small new direction to your life? 'Don't be ridiculous!' you may well be thinking, and if so, then you need to wake up and smell the coffee, because you are as much open to influence as anyone else. Now before you start to think that being influenced means something negative, in most cases it isn't – some of the greatest views, thoughts, and feelings you are ever going to have will have started out by someone else planting their own insights into your mind. But just every now and then, being influenced has a definite downside.

Nicky didn't want to be friends with Tammy any more because Tammy wasn't a believer and they didn't share the same views on life. She realised that she was being influenced by Tammy and for the sake of her faith she wanted out. You, most likely, have more friends who aren't Christians than those who are, but that doesn't mean you need to do what Nicky did. It does mean, though, that you need to check what influence they are having on you. You are influenced by every friendship, and the question is: is the influence positive or negative? Are you doing things you know to be wrong, do you find yourself being tempted more when you are with certain friends? Does your girl or boyfriend push you to do things you are uncomfortable with? Are you more likely to get drunk or get into a fight, or be more negative and gossipy when out with certain mates? The real question is: how comfortable would you be, doing whatever you were doing, if you could actually see Jesus face to face at the same time? If the answer is that you wouldn't be relaxed or at ease, then something is not right and has to change for the better!

However, what Nicky missed out on was the fact that she could have influenced her friend for good. She could actually have been a great witness to Tammy. The way she ended up dealing with her non-Christian friend was hardly going to have her running to church the following Sunday! The way you act and respond in your relationships can turn things right round. You have the opportunity to get in the driving seat: don't be a pushover, don't say 'yes' too quickly, but be an example that has your friends, family, girl or boyfriend intrigued as to what goes on inside that head of yours!

On the other hand, don't be dumb either. If you're being negatively influenced then you might need to press the ejector seat button and bail out. Peter wrote, 'So then, dear friends ... make every effort to be found spotless, blameless and at peace with him' (2 Peter 3:14). In other words, don't get messed up with wrong stuff, but keep yourself clean and right with God.

Noone should have to tell you who your friends are going to be or who you should go out with. Nobody should have to tell you that you have changed for the worse, because with God's help and an active conscience you should already know. Relationships should be great, they should keep you happy and continually change your life for the better. Make sure your relationships are doing just that!

Radical Action Guide

How to keep a good relationship:
1. Pray about it – if they are Christians pray with them, if they aren't then pray for them.
2. Check yourself regularly as to whether you are being influenced in a wrong way.
3. Check yourself regularly as to how you are influencing others.
4. Be as loving, caring, and giving as you can be.
5. Be encouraging, warm, and friendly.
6. Be honest and truthful.
7. Be forgiving and patient.
8. Take time to talk with each other, but make sure you listen too.
9. Be sensitive and understanding.
10. Always give your friend plenty of space, as well as making time for your own space and for other relationships.

Relationships & their influence

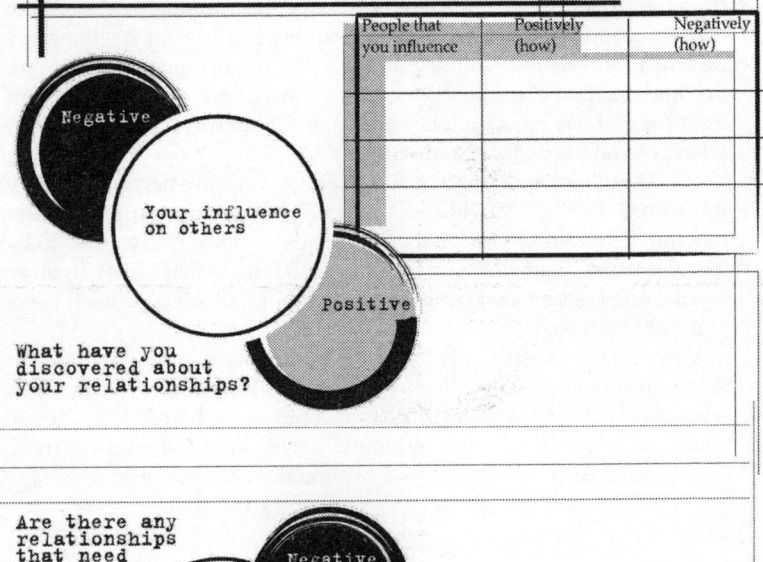

What have you discovered about your relationships?

Are there any relationships that need to change?

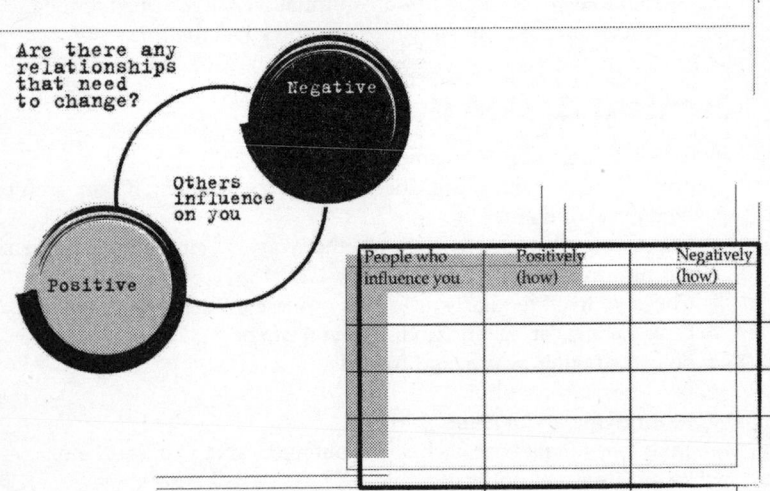

Think it through...

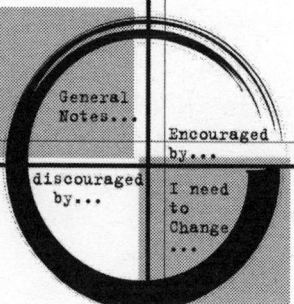

General Notes...

Encouraged by...

discouraged by...

I need to Change...

EVALUATE

✓ Get it RIGHT!

Sex

The big issue

They hadn't been going out longer than three months, but Peter and Sophie felt pretty much in love. He was eighteen and she had just turned seventeen. Everyone was telling them how good they looked together; things were going really well. After seeing a film at the cinema and grabbing a bag of chips from the chippie to eat on the way home, Sophie brought the conversation round to sex. 'Peter, I really love you and I'm happier with you than I've ever been with anyone else. There is just one thing left that would make our relationship perfect. I think we should start sleeping together.'

Peter thought for a while before responding. 'Sophie you're really attractive, and getting turned on when I'm with you is certainly no problem. I love you just as much as you love me. But just because we want to sleep with each other doesn't mean we should.' Surprised, she asked him why. He paused for a moment and before he could say anything, Sophie asked if it was to do with the fact he was a Christian. He just nodded. 'OK, Peter, I can go along with that. I don't really understand it, but I respect you.' A few months later Peter and Sophie broke up; she wanted to end it and told him so over the phone. Gutted, Peter asked her the reason, and without hesitating, Sophie told him in a gentle but firm voice, 'Peter, we had something going, the no-sex thing was kind of cool and refreshing for a while, but I want to have sex, I want to enjoy life. You might want to be a monk or something but I don't want to be a nun!' With that, she said goodbye and put the phone down.

Talking point

♦ Do you think Peter was right to say, no?

♦ What does not having sex have to do with being a Christian?

- Sophie wasn't a Christian and didn't understand his views. Do you think it's a good or bad idea for Christians to go out with people who don't have the same belief or faith?
- Do you agree with the 'no sex before you're married' rule in Christianity, or do you think it's a little old-fashioned and outdated, no longer relevant?
- If you were in Peter's shoes, do you think it would be easy for you to say 'no' like he did?

Bible point

Sex is for marriage.
'For this reason a man will leave his father and mother and be united to his wife, and they will become one flesh' Genesis 2:24.

Sex is to be enjoyed.
'May you rejoice in the wife of your youth' Proverbs 5:18.

Sex is to be enjoyed by two people for life.
'Marriage should be honoured by all, and the marriage bed kept pure, for God will judge the adulterer and all the sexually immoral' Hebrews 13:4.

Sex before marriage is not what God intend for us.
'It is God's will that you should be sanctified (holy): that you should avoid sexual immorality; that each of you should learn to control your own body in a way that is holy and honourable, not in passionate lust like the heathen' 1 Thessalonians 4:3-5.

Sex can begin before the bedroom.
'But I tell you that anyone who looks at a woman lustfully has already committed adultery with her in his heart' Matthew 5:28.

Listening point

You've just made the biggest catch of your life – the most gorgeous girl or guy is going out with you. You go to see a movie or to a club, this person is so exciting to be with. On the way back home you start to kiss: it's good, in fact it's great, after twenty minutes of snogging you really want to go back to your bedroom. You are so turned on and this person makes you feel fantastic, every fibre of your body is urging you to sleep with this hunk or babe!

If you've ever felt like that, there is nothing actually wrong with it. In fact, if you didn't feel that way then you were either seeing a brick or someone you didn't really like.

Sex is in your face almost all the time – you see a film, watch TV, read a book, pick up a magazine, speak with a friend, and it's either being talked about, referred to, or you see it – sure, you may not see the act, but the imagery is enough! It makes you think everyone is doing it all the time. Well, we know that's not quite true but pretty much everyone is doing it at some time. The reality is that a good number of your friends have either had sex or played around in a sexual way with their girl or boyfriends. You have probably heard all about it! There are people you will have met (though you may not know it) who first did it when they were as young as eleven or twelve! If you're a guy and over the age of twelve, then, like every other guy, you think about it and would love to do it (a bit nervous maybe but still …)! If you're a girl, perhaps you're not as eager – and sure you're nervous about getting pregnant – but sex is not a million miles from your thoughts – with the right guy. For that matter, sex is not exactly a million miles from the thoughts of any living, feeling human who has sexual organs! But as a teenager, your desire is more intense than someone in their thirties, in fact you may feel like your emotions are totally out of control!

So when you're in youth group or on the back row in church and you're staring at or secretly holding hands with the most adorable person in the place, feelings may like burst as your youth leader or, your minister drops the depression bomb and tells you 'Christians don't have sex before marriage!' It seems like saying, 'Christians don't eat'. You were made to have sex, you don't need a biology lesson to learn that; the first book in the Bible points that out. So how come you mustn't do it – at least until you're almost too old to do it, that is?

Well, there are good reasons why not. You might not like them, you might not want to agree with them, but they do make sense.

1. Sex is more than a good time – It isn't just a 'wow' experience, or a 'same time next week' kind of thing. Sure, it may be that way for some, but there is much more to it than that. Every time two people have sex something happens way beyond the physical stuff. One night Alex does it with Kim and the next night he gets Anna; some may say, 'Good for him!' Why not, if that's all you know? But the truth is we do actually know better. We know sleeping around is abusing any real relationship so that a person becomes just a sexy well-shaped object to have fun with for a night. Forget the personality, the laughs, and the friendship, 'just do it' and go on to the next one! That may well be the way the rest of the world thinks it should be done, but it's not right. Nor is it right to do it outside marriage with the person you love and are really serious about. From a biblical point of view sex is for marriage only. 'How come?' you may wonder. It's because, whenever you do it, it's such an amazing act that there isn't just unbelievable chemistry going on to give you a night to remember, other things are happening, too. The Bible tells us we bond with that person – but it isn't a bond for the evening, so that you want to cuddle the person afterwards, it's a lifetime bond. God created sex so that when two people do it, it actually strengthens their relationship by knitting them together so they become one person! It's an act for just one relationship throughout life, to bless it, transform it, and enrich it (Genesis 2:24). So if a person sleeps around, every time he or she moves on, there is a bond being ripped apart at a spiritual and emotional level we will never really understand.

2. Sex has a lasting touch – When a married couple have been around the block together and seen each other's weary faces every morning when they don't exactly look their best, when they have had just about enough of each other's irritating habits such as gassing the bedroom out, and they have heard all the stories and jokes a hundred times over, it doesn't mean the relationship is over. It isn't time to trade the person in for a better model with more mod cons and less rattles (Hebrews 13:4). The exact opposite is true – the marriage has matured. The relationship is moving on into a whole new undiscovered level of deep intimate friendship. Sex is an active part of keeping relationships going and moving when the so-called spice is on the way out. 'Making love' contributes to bringing it back – actually this involves more than sex but it is something special that God has given to help. In God's view, there is no room for a third person to make the bored and unsatisfied wife or husband find a spark again. They don't need to look beyond their own bedroom walls to find that! Sex is for two people and two people only throughout life.

3. Sex is for expressing love and making a family – In other words sex actually procreates! When you really love someone you want to be with them and that usually involves forming a family (Genesis 9:1). That family is born out of love, and that child is a physical image of two people's love. What if your relationship resulted in a pregnancy by mistake? Would you do the 'honourable thing' and stay with the person for life, trying to make it work? Would you split up, knowing that there is a child somewhere who will grow up realising they physically represent two people who don't love each other any more (or never really did)? Or would you have an abortion? Principles and beliefs about life and death can so easily be sidelined in times of crisis. Imagine if it happened? It would be your worst nightmare, and no matter how good the sex was, would it really be worth a lifetime of heartache and guilt? This is not what God has in mind for you and your future family!

4. Sex is for amateurs – So you lose your virginity, sure, it might have felt good for you, but was it good for the other person? Were you as good as the last person they did it with? Did they leave you a present they had picked up somewhere else, like a sexual disease? Condoms may reduce the risk of disease but they are far from 100 per cent safe. When you do finally find the person of your dreams, will they be as good as the others you've had it with? Will you love them for who they are 95 per cent of the day, and then underneath the sheets find yourself thinking back to some ex-boy or girlfriend who made sex ultra-amazing? Imagine it, you're married and every time it comes to the love stuff you're disappointed because you just wish that extra little something you had elsewhere could be found. Marriage and sex are not supposed to involve rivalry, in other words the only way to enjoy it fully is to be innocent with the lover of your dreams. Start out together and that way you'll never know any difference, because together you will work it out until it's fantastic. No intimidation, embarrassment, resentment, or memories to hinder the two of you – just plenty of innocent love and fun! The only way of guaranteeing that is by waiting till your wedding day.

OK, that makes sense, but it doesn't help. It just makes you feel guilty because you want to *do* it, or perhaps because you are discovering the Christian viewpoint a little too late. Isn't it actually impossible not to do it? Sure, it's possible, but all the same it's a real tough issue dealing with the electrifying and compelling desire to do it with someone who turns you on. How can you control how you feel and stop going too far when the heat is really on?

Here is a suggested guideline. It may look stupid, it may look ridiculous but behind it is simple practical common sense. Your every aim with that hotshot babe or hunk should be to stop yourself getting turned on (and if you're turned on, then dealing with it quickly and effectively). That can be done in all sorts of ways, such as avoiding danger areas like bedrooms, choosing to being with others rather than on your own together, and being careful how long you kiss for. Don't reject the list straight out (or another list of guidelines your youth leader has given you) because those who do are far more likely to miss the warning signs and then after that it can often be too late.

Christians are not immune from failing in the heat of the moment and actually having sex. If that's you and you have either fooled around in a way you know isn't right, or had full-blown sex, then you probably also know that what you did is not what God had in mind for you to do. In other words you have sinned; first and foremost it's wrong and you need to be aware of that. However, you are certainly not alone and there are two things you should know.

First, that God loves you just as much now as he did before and second, that God can forgive you as easily as he forgave you for anything else you have ever done. There are also two things you need to do.

Most importantly you need to get right with God again and the way you do that is by telling him what you did and that you are sorry (if you are) and you wish you hadn't done it, and then ask for his forgiveness. The next thing is you should speak with someone you trust such as a youth leader or your minister. They can help you to deal with any guilt you may have, and also help and advise you on how best to deal with the relationship you have or had with the person you had sex with. Their prayers and advice will help you to receive the healing that only God can give. Guilt following a previous sexual relationship can be removed, so that when you do find the person of your dreams the wedding day will not be tainted in any way, either for you or your partner. Nor will it affect the rest of your married life.

Make a decision to wait like Peter did regardless of the consequences. Be disciplined and keep to your guidelines, because one day you will have a partner with whom you can share and enjoy yourself at the deepest of levels and know it's an experience nobody else has shared with either of you. That is definitely something worth waiting for and it's also something for which God will bless the two of you in a big way. Be different, be radical – give it a miss for now!

Radical Action guide

In your relationship make sure of these things
1. Pray with each other regularly, by praying you are allowing God to be involved in the relationship.
2. Go public so that everyone knows you are a couple and there is no secrecy.
3. Be sure that your boy/girlfriend holds the same spiritual values as you do. You stand a greater chance of making things work; as two Christians, rather than having one person not sharing the same views or feelings (like Peter and Sophie).
4. Don't be exclusive, make sure other people can hang around with you and that both you and they feel comfortable.

5. If you're into kissing then go ahead! But keep it under control, a fifteen minute snogging session certainly turns on the heat. When either of you starts to get turned on it's time to turn off! But in truth, you should have turned off way before the turn-on point! Be practical, give yourself no more than one or two minutes of kissing at any time. Many people far cleverer than I am believe that intimate kissing should not be practiced until marriage, for the same reasons as for sex, as well as the fact kissing is a form of foreplay. By not kissing, you reduce the temptation, and keep the heat down. That is something for you to think about and decide for yourself, it is a valuable point.
6. Keep off what you don't have – In other words exploring hands on your boy or girlfriend's body should be a real big 'no, no!' It's a major turn on, and it's called 'foreplay'. It may not be intercourse but it is sex!
7. Private space in public places – It's really important in your relationship that you get time together, but be sure it's not in places like bedrooms where doors are closed. In the wrong setting a spark is sure to ignite a fire you will not want to put out. Protect yourselves by being in places where other people are nearby, so you won't be able to do anything embarrassing or that you may regret.
8. Dress to please, not to kill. If you wear really tight and revealing clothes where virtually nothing is left to the imagination, whether you intend it or not, two things are happening: you are sure to excite your partner and you are giving him or her a 'come-on' signal. Be trendy and look great but draw the line.

the Sex issue...
Expectations

Her/My...   Our...   His/My...

Take a look at the list below and decide which of these things are your decision, your girl or boy friends decision or your joint decision as a couple. Some things may actually be both of your decisions but not a joint one. Some of the items on the list you may not see as appropriate and not include at all, though there may be some things you wish to add. Simply insert them in the box and then in the correct places next to the illustrations above

Take the lead	Talk about issues	Talk with my parents
Make the decisions	Talk about feelings/desires	Talk with his/her parents
Set the guidelines	Decide on boudaries	Talk with your youth leader
Make the moves	Pray about issues & feelings	Be honest when things get too hot
Say Yes or No to the physical stuff like kissing, cuddling & holding hands	Be willing to open be open and discuss the relationship with others	Be honest when things get too cold

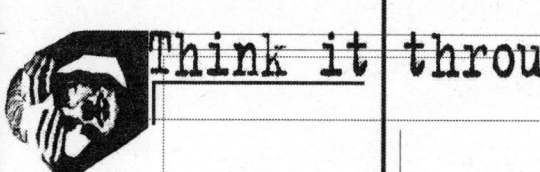
Think it through...

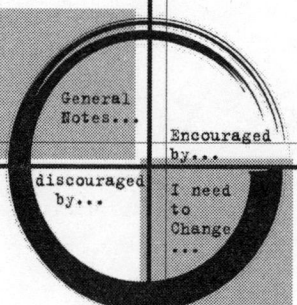

General Notes...
Encouraged by...
discouraged by...
I need to Change...

EVALUATE
✓ Get it RIGHT!

Temptation

The big issue

Fiona had never once skipped school, she had hardly ever taken a day off sick either. Her parents were fairly strict and she only ever got a day off if she was nearly at death's door, vomiting, and with a temperature of over a 100°F to prove it. Then, and only then, was she allowed a day off! Fiona was in her last term before her GCSE final exams. She had studied as hard as she could. The sight of yet another text book made her feel instantly sick, and she feels the voice of another teacher droning on about the importance of persevering with her studies was sure to make her snap. So she needed little persuasion when her best friend Hayley asked her to skip school and spend the day in town shopping, or getting drunk or something else rebellious. She wasn't so keen about getting drunk, but to escape school seemed an excellent idea, only she felt nervous because she had never missed a day before. 'Is it that easy?' she wondered. Hayley assured her everything would be fine and the following day she left home in school uniform, with her normal school bag full of clothes to change into. She met Hayley and they headed off for the bus stop, this time on the opposite side of the road to all her school mates. They didn't have to wait long before the bus came and took the two of them into town where they found a public toilet and changed. They spent the morning browsing in the shops until at 11.30 as they were walking through the shopping mall, they were stopped by a police officer and another man in plain clothes. The police officer said nothing as the other guy, wearing a tasteless brown suit, and a sickly smile, introduced himself as the local truant officer. Before he could finish speaking Hayley announced that she was sixteen, had left school, and was currently looking for a job. Fiona knew the only way out was to lie. 'Yeah, me too!' she said somewhat unconvincingly. 'OK, let me take a few details,' the guy said with his smile spreading further across his face. Without any warning and to Fiona's complete surprise, Hayley shouted, 'Run!'

and tore off down the mall. Fiona hesitated for a split second, then as she began to move, a large hand seized her arm. 'No you don't, Miss!' declared the police officer. Less than an hour later, Fiona's father arrived to collect her from the police station. He looked as if he was about to explode. Without introducing himself to either the truant officer or the police officer, he brushed past both of them as though they weren't there. Looking into his daughter's eyes, and speaking through his teeth, he said, 'You've dragged our name in the mud – you deceive us by playing truant from school, you lie to the police and then try to run away. Don't you care about your exams? Don't you care about the law? Don't you even care how this makes your mum or me feel?' Fiona looked away, wishing she'd never got out of bed that morning.

Talking point

- What was Fiona's first mistake?
- How would you define the word 'temptation'?
- Have you ever found yourself in a situation like Fiona, giving into temptation and then getting into trouble? What happened?
- Have you ever tempted other people to do something which got them into trouble? How?
- What is your most common temptation?
- How do you deal with temptation?
- Do you think temptation can ever be good? Why do you think so?

Bible point

Genesis 3:1 – *'Now the serpent was more crafty than any other of the wild animals the Lord God had made. He said to the woman, "Did God really say, 'You must not eat from any tree in the garden'?"*

If you've ever wondered where all the problems in the world started from, the answer is here. Up to this point Adam and Eve loved God and walked with him; the world was great, no disease, no pain – there wasn't even death. But one simple twisted question, causing doubt and temptation, ended this life of beauty and perfection. Now we live in a world damaged by sin and corruption, with all kinds of evil plaguing our everyday living. And all because two people gave in to the simplest of temptations. We all face temptations of various kinds every, day but we should realize that even the smallest things are able to cause great harm. It's unlikely that whatever you give into will affect the rest of the world, but it could hurt someone else; it could even hurt you eventually!

Mark 14:10,11 – *'Then Judas Iscariot, one of the Twelve, went to the chief priests to betray Jesus to them. They were delighted to hear this and promised to give him money. So he watched for an opportunity to hand him over'*

Judas had been tempted to go against Jesus, to hand him over to his enemies, and make some money out of it in the process. When we feel tempted, it nearly always involves either personal gain using unfair methods, or rebellion against someone or something. Judas' temptation was to bring down Jesus, but, as is often the case, the exact opposite happened and the only lasting downfall was that of Judas Iscariot.

Matthew 4:2-4 – *'After fasting forty days and forty nights, he was hungry. The tempter came to him and said, "If you are the Son of God, tell these stones to become bread." Jesus answered, "It is written: 'People do not live on bread alone, but on every word that comes from the mouth of God.'"'*

Jesus was tired and hungry and Satan tried to exploit this weakness. But even then Jesus would not give in to the temptation. We should realize that the devil finds our weakest points and provides us with many opportunities to give in. Temptation is not in itself wrong, in fact it's quite normal, but what counts is how you respond to it. Jesus simply whacked the ball back into the devil's court.

Listening point

When you've finished your essay on the computer and your three year-old brother or sister pulls out the power lead by mistake, wiping out all your work, doesn't that make you scream with rage? When you're waiting at a bus stop, desperate to get home, and the bus goes past without stopping although it's almost empty, have you never been provoked into making a gesture at the no-good driver? When you're speaking on the phone to your friend, and your mum or dad picks up the other phone and tells you to get off the line because they wish to make a call, no doubt you've felt like using four-letter words to express your frustration at their blatant insensitivity. These are kinds of temptation we face every day – as well as other stuff like bunking off school or work, throwing all the dirty dishes in the bin when it's your turn to wash up, or twisting the truth about the homework you were set to do three weeks ago but which is still unfinished.

When the opportunity for something better or more enjoyable comes your way, should you take it without a second thought? The temptation could be a quick way to get cash with no questions asked, or the chance to drop someone in it for what they did to you, or perhaps the opportunity to dodge your responsibilities. Whatever it is, it seems desirable at the time, but later may blow up in your face – in other words, it has repercussions.

We've already seen how King David's desire to sleep with a beautiful woman got him into a real mess, and we've just looked at Judas who traded in Jesus for cash and ended up hanging himself. Your temptation may not be as drastic as either of these were but neither was Fiona's temptation to take a day off school. Yet it still went horribly wrong for her. Very likely you've been there and done that. You've learned the hard way that things often don't go to plan. So often you've been found out. That great idea never really worked or if it did, either you still feel guilty or you're always looking behind you. Maybe you don't feel guilty, but you probably should, because most of the time when we give into temptation we are doing something wrong. In other words we are sinning, and if we are sinning we are rebelling against what God wants for us. Unless you have asked for his forgiveness then there is something in your life that God needs and wants to deal with big or small, either way. It may be it's still an issue between you and him.

The Bible has many names for the devil and one of them is 'the tempter'. He knows what it is that will make your hardest resistance weaken. But that doesn't mean you are always bound to give in and fall flat on your face. If you 'resist the devil then he will flee from you' (James 4:7). So ignore whatever he puts into your head – don't feed it by thinking about it, just starve it by switching your attention to something else.

If, for example, a sexual thought suddenly drops into your mind from nowhere, don't get hung up on it and worry that it's a sin, don't even give it the time of day. If you dwell on such thoughts and begin to fantasize about all sorts of sexual things, or if your dreams progress into sexual activities, then sure enough that is sin. But if you ignore it and focus on something else, then you have done absolutely nothing wrong and have no reason to feel bad. It should disappear and you can get on with your life.

The most destructive weapon known to man is certainly not the nuclear bomb, not biological or chemical warfare, not large amounts of cash, not even a revealing picture of the most gorgeous babe or hunk that is sure to send you wild. No, it's the smallest seed of temptation planted into the weak areas of your life. Sex, greed, and power usually lie at the root of all temptation. Watch out, because temptation often comes in subtle, quiet, and unassuming ways, but it has the ability to change your life and that the people around you radically. Like any seed, if it's watered, it grows and spreads out its roots. The bigger it gets, the harder it is to remove. Resist your seed of temptation straight away, and there won't be any plants that you will be forced to try and remove later on. It's as simple as that!

Radical Action Guide

When you're struggling with temptation –
1. Ignore it.
2. Change your environment or focus.
3. Pray about it.
4. Talk to someone you trust about how you are feeling, ask them to pray with you regularly.
5. Have a person watch out for you who will give you guidelines on how to prevent the temptation turning into action. For example, if you have problems with sexual thoughts, keep out of newsagents where you've spotted porno. Stay away from watching indecent videos or TV programmes.

If the temptation increases in intensity –
6. Confess any previous sin where you have failed in that area before.
7. Speak to your youth leader or minister and have them pray through areas of your life where previous sins have left their roots.

If the temptation becomes too much and you give in to it –
8. Always remember God loves you and understands.
9. Always remember that God can and does forgive you when you fail, if you ask for forgiveness.
10. Always remember you are his child and he will hold you, even when you fall.

the Temptation Board

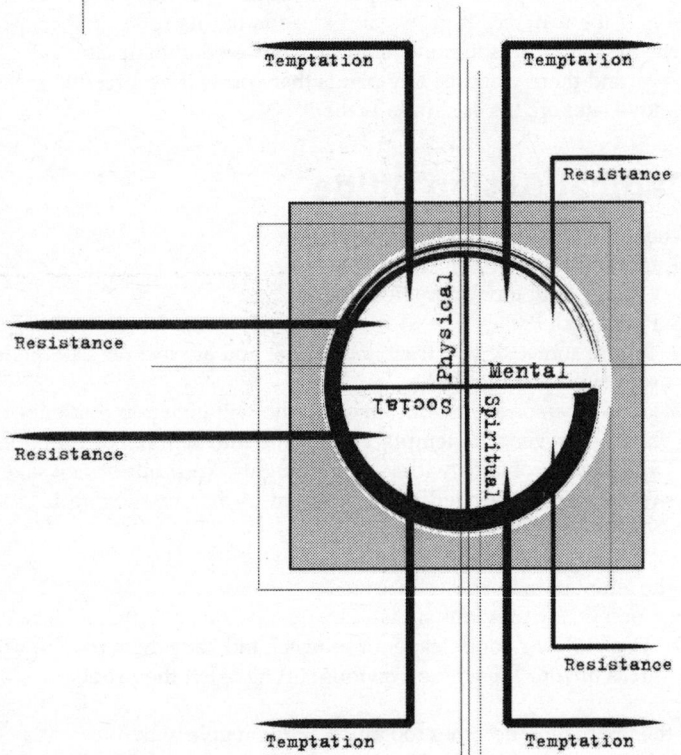

Take a look at the four areas of your life and then place next to each designated line what your biggest temptation is in that particular area. Then write on the following line how you most effectively combat or resist that temptation.

After you have finished, ask yourself whether you are gaining or losing ground in the four areas of temptation you have question.

Think it through...

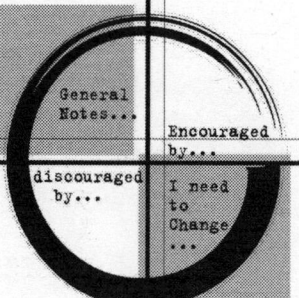

General Notes...
Encouraged by...
discouraged by...
I need to Change...

EVALUATE
✓ Get it RIGHT!

Understanding

The big issue

They met each other in casualty. Mel had twisted her ankle, or possibly broken it, she couldn't be sure which, since she hadn't yet been seen. Luke had already been seen and was waiting to be seen again. Both were in wheelchairs sitting next to each other. 'Does it hurt?' Luke asked, without really needing to hear the answer.

'Of course it hurts!' barked Mel, insulted he might be implying she was faking it. Then she realized her response had been quite harsh and unfair.

'What did you do?' he asked.

'Wow, he's eager!' Mel thought to herself, and then told him the story of how she had fallen over in a hockey game. Softened, Mel asked Luke why he was waiting in casualty – there was no obvious reason. 'I blacked out at home,' he explained.

'How come?' Mel followed up, now rather more interested. She noticed that a change had come over him; he looked down at his feet and seemed to go a little pale.

'Well, err … I have a brain tumour.' She barely heard him say it because he was now mumbling, and it was hard to see, but it looked as if his chin was trembling. Tears were not far off.

Mel felt a little awkward for and now wished she hadn't asked. 'Yeah, but you're going to be OK, right? I mean, they're giving you all the treatment you need?' Mel too had lost her confidence, her questions were bumbly and there was tension in the air.

'No … I don't have too long left. I turned down the treatment, I was sick of it. It made me puke all the time, I lost my hair.' For the first time, Mel noticed that his hair had a slightly unnatural look about it. 'Oh, it's a wig,' she thought. He went on, 'I hated every moment of it – all the therapy and the tests. Each time hearing that the treatment wasn't working. So that's an end of it.'

Now Mel spotted a tear. In the anxiety of the moment, she said something she later regretted. 'But, isn't it dangerous to stop the therapy? I mean won't you die if you don't keep it up?' Peter lifted his head slightly, enough to be able to see her. The two made eye contact. He didn't reply, he didn't have to. Their conversation ended, neither knowing what else to say. Eventually Mel was called and wheeled away to be examined.

Talking point

- Did Mel show any signs of sensitivity or of being a help to Luke in his distress?

- How would you have dealt with the situation if you were Mel?

- Most people are not very good at dealing with awkward situations, and either change the conversation or stop talking altogether. Is that always a good thing? Explain your answer.

- What do you think Luke really needed from Mel?

- Has there ever been a time in your life when you have been ill, lost a member of your family or one of your friends, or had a boy/girlfriend dump you etc? What did you need most from your friends at that time?

- Has any one ever confided in you about a problem or a hurt that they had? How did you respond?

- What is involved in being sensitive and trying to understand someone's problems?

Bible point

Understanding involves the ability to relate.
'When Jesus saw her weeping, and the Jews who had come along with her also weeping, he was deeply moved in spirit and troubled' John 11:33.

Understanding involves listening.
'Everyone should be quick to listen, slow to speak and slow to become angry' James 1:19.

Understanding involves compassion.
'I will set out and go back to my father and say to him, "Father I have sinned against heaven and against you. I am no longer worthy to be called your son;

make me like one of your hired men." So he got up and went to his father. But while he was still a long way off, his father saw him and was filled with compassion for him; he ran to his son, threw his arms around him and kissed him' Luke 15:18-20.

Listening point

'You just don't understand!' That is one of the most frequently used phrases you will find in a house where teenagers live. Many teenagers spend alot of time either feeling lonely or with other emotions that nobody else seems to understand. (If they do understand, they certainly don't show it!)

However, being a teenager dealing with many of the issues that you face, some of which we have already explored, can mean that it is sometimes difficult to get a handle on other people's feelings. When someone starts to go on about their 'little' problem, you may think, 'That's nothing, wait until I tell you what's going on with me!' Or you can't wait for them to stop moaning so you can give them the advice that they obviously need! But, actually, you are in a far better position than most people to make a huge impact on the person who has the problem, however big or small it may be. Why? Because you know what it's like to hurt, or feel isolated and alone. But – and this is a big BUT – that doesn't mean you have to tell them about what's happened to you. The truth is that, within two minutes of listening to a person, most people have actually stopped listening and started giving them the 'answer' to their problems. Which usually isn't what they want or need. What they really want is for you to listen *without* speaking, to show concern and offer a hug (that is if you're a girl, and if you're a guy *do* whatever it is you *do* to show you care for another bloke).

What Luke certainly did not need was Mel's quick reply, 'Isn't that dangerous?' He took this to mean, 'Are you brain dead? Have you even thought about this?' Nor did he need Mel's awkward silence, which followed when the impact of his diagnosis hit her. He didn't even want Mel to feel sorry for him. He simply needed a friend, someone he could talk to about how hard it was and with whom he could share his fears and worries – even talk about death and what he thought it would be like (if he was ready for that, for not everyone reaches that stage). For her part, Mel could have offered him three valuable things and gained a friend.
1. She had a chance to show loving concern to someone who really needed it.

2. The chance to share her beliefs about God, life, and the hope he could have.
3. And also a chance to pray for him. Not necessarily with him (although that could happen). But she could even pray that he would be healed (that also could happen). And she could at least pray about how he was feeling and about his worries, his pain and the time he had left. All this, of course, would take longer than five minutes in casualty, but if they were to become friends, there would be more time.

Do you begin to get it? If a person just stops to listen and tries to understand the other person, they are handed an opportunity on a plate to help someone in a huge way. This isn't just for the likes of Luke or someone else who may be dying. But it's for anyone – a friend whose parents are getting divorced, someone who's just got the sack at work, someone who's being bullied, or your best mate who's been dumped from the football team, or worse – a girlfriend or boyfriend. If you just listen, it's amazing what people will say, and it's even more amazing what you can do for them. But too often we don't listen because we are caught up in our own problems, and when we don't listen, we miss the chance possibly to change the course of someone's life.

One day Jesus met the local tax collector, a man called Zacchaeus, he went round to his house and had a meal with him. Everyone was mad with Jesus for doing that; Zacchaeus was not a nice guy, he stole from people. When people couldn't afford to pay their tax, nor the commission he took for himself, he simply took the money by force or set the law on them. People detested him. But Jesus saw a different Zacchaeus to the one everyone else saw. When he went round to his home, he had every opportunity to set Zacchaeus straight. Yet over the course of the night there is no mention of Jesus saying anything; apparently he just listened to him, and by the time they parted, Zacchaeus confessed everything and wanted to undo all that he had done wrong. Then Jesus said, 'Today salvation has come to this house' (Luke 19:9).

What had happened that caused Zacchaeus to change his ways and receive eternal life, even though Jesus didn't say anything? Had Jesus barged in to Zacchaeus' house and told him he was a sinner and a thief and that he needed to 'turn or burn', Zacchaeus might have been put off and the opportunity of his life would have been lost. The very same principle applies to people who haven't done anything wrong but are struggling with problems. Through talking about it, they often see what to do next. Not because you said anything but because they heard the answer in what they said themselves. That's why these words in James 1:19 are so important, 'Be quick to listen, slow to speak.'

Be a friend to those in need by being quick to listen, and when you listen, try to see things as if you were in their shoes. Once you've related to them, be slow to speak, and show by your actions that you have compassion, and that you have understood their need. There are times when we need to speak and give advice, but be wise about when you do it and what you say. As Christians, we want to help change our world. The easiest place to start is by lending an ear and listening to a mate or even a stranger who's got a problem!

Radical Action Guide

When someone has something to say –
1. Stop thinking about things that are more important to you and give them your full attention.
2. Try and see things from their point of view.
3. Bite your tongue when you think you see an obvious answer or when you just want to tell them to stop being stupid.
4. Give them encouraging signs that you are still listening and that you understand.
5. If you don't understand, say in a non-threatening and non-judgmental way that you don't get it.
6. If they ask you, then share your thoughts, but rather than giving them answers ask them questions and see if they can get the drift of where you are going.
7. Try and be positive, but remember that there is nothing more irritating than someone telling you to see the bright side of life, or taking the opposite viewpoint. They want and need an ally; but on the other hand, don't trap yourself into a position you might regret later.
8. Pray for them and if you are able to, pray with them.
9. Keep on being their friend, and be willing to listen even if it drags on and you're losing patience.
10. Ask God for wisdom about how to respond to a problem that seems to have no solution.

Discovering
the ART of REAL Understanding

Am I good at Listening?

	Always	Sometimes	Never
Do I like to hog the conversations more than i like to listen?	5	3	1
When someone starts to talk so I immediately start listening?	5	3	1
When the juicy bits in the conversation are over or there isn't any juice, do I get bored quickly?	5	3	1
Do I get frustrated when people talk for a long time?	5	3	1
Do I want to butt in and give them the answers to all their problems?	5	3	1
Do I only listen carefully to people I really like?	5	3	1
Do I make judgments about people as they talk?	5	3	1
If things get a little uncomfortable, embarrassing or awkward do I stop the conversation or change direction?	5	3	1
Do I get put off listening if they start to waffle?	5	3	1
If I can't relate to the problem do I switch off?	5	3	1

Circle the points in each column where appropriate

Combined Total=

If you scored
- 15 or less - You are a great listener and people will find it easy to talk to you
- 30-16 - Yeah you can listen if you have to but there is work to be done
- 50-31 - Sorry to say it, but you are an awful listener. People may talk to you but what's the point?

1. What did the above diagram tell you about what kind of listener you are?

2. Do you feel it is a true indicator or not? Why?

3. Are there things you know you need to work on?

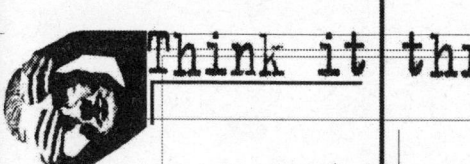
Think it through...

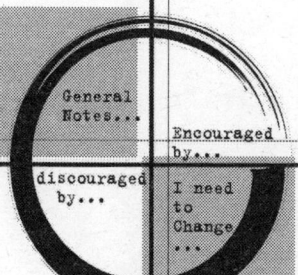

General Notes...	Encouraged by...
discouraged by...	I need to Change ...

EVALUATE

✓ Get it RIGHT!

Videos

The big issue

Most Friday nights Ebun would roll back to his parents' house after a club or party with several bags of food from the local Chinese, a couple of mates, and a video. If his parents were still up they quickly took their leave.

This particular Friday seemed to be going like any other. The food was fine, his friends were desperately trying to sober up from the party, and the film seemed decent enough. Usually Ebun preferred a violent 'blood and guts' film, but this evening it was Tom who had chosen the video. It was a 'horror' but they were blokes and it would take a fair bit to freak them – or so they thought. Just 30 minutes of flesh being torn, spirits with twisted and distorted figures appearing at random, and the creepiest of music was enough for each of them to close their eyes and wish that Tom had chosen Jackie Chan instead. At the end of 45 minutes Ebun was ready to be sick, Tom was so pale he certainly looked as if he was going to be sick, and Marc watched on hoping the video recorder would suddenly chew the tape up and spit it out. No such luck. Since each of them was too proud and macho to stop the tape, they watched on. After the film had finished, the three sat in silence. Ebun was too afraid to get up and go to the toilet for fear of meeting something nasty, while Tom and Marc didn't really want to walk home at 1.30 in the morning, especially since it meant passing a graveyard. Each of them remained still, comforted by the others' company, watching time go by and waiting for day to break. By 6.30 the sun began to rise. Ebun felt it was now safe to head for the toilet, almost unable to walk with the pain. On his return, he discovered the other two fast asleep for the first time that night. Now it was light, nothing would happen to them.

Talking Point

- What is your reaction to Ebun and his friends?

- Do you think we should be careful about what we watch, read or hear? Explain your answer?

- Have you ever watched, read, or listened to something that has had a long-lasting negative impact upon you?

- Do you think that a person should follow the age restrictions placed on a film?

- Even if a person is over the age of eighteen should they watch a film with an 18-certificate knowing it will contain strong violence, nudity, bad language, or psychological stress?

- Do you think Christians should avoid a film if its content includes any of the following categories: ✓(or ✗)

☐ Romance
☐ Thrillers
☐ Bad language
☐ Religious
☐ New Age
☐ Emotionally challenging
☐ Low morals and principles

☐ Animation
☐ Fantasy
☐ Science fiction
☐ Horror
☐ Music
☐ Period (thematic)

☐ Violence
☐ Sex & Nudity
☐ Supernatural
☐ Action
☐ Racism
☐ Mystery
☐ Corruption & Greed

Your own suggestions:-

♦ What kind of magazines do you think Christians should avoid (✓ or ✗) and why?

☐ Gossip magazines
☐ Sexually explicit articles
☐ Agony columns
☐ Superstition/supernatural (e.g. star signs)
☐ Pornographic pictures
☐ Romance
☐ Scandal
☐ New Age

Your own suggestions:

♦ If there are any types of music you think are bad for you to listen to name them and give your reasons.

♦ Do you think people should be allowed to watch, listen to, or read whatever they want to? Why do you think so?

Bible point

Philippians 4:8 – *'Finally, brothers and sisters, whatever is true, whatever is noble, whatever is right, whatever is pure, whatever is lovely, whatever is admirable – if anything is excellent or praiseworthy – think about such things'*
What a verse! But what does it actually mean? Well, it's saying that rather than fill our heads and lives with things that are destructive for us, we should focus on the things that are positive and good. As Christians we want to live a life as much like Jesus as possible. If our heads are full of images and thoughts that contain violence, sex, foul language, low morality, deceit, and satanic or evil impressions, then we are being pulled in the wrong direction. But if we feed our minds only on things that build us up, we will find his path easier to walk in.

Romans 12:2 – *'Do not conform any longer to the pattern of this world, but be transformed by the renewing of your mind. Then you will be able to test and approve what God's will is – his good, pleasing and perfect will'*
While you are nuking some city or other on the PC or games console, or you're listening to music lyrics which describe just how great orgasms

are, or you're watching some zombie or other rip out the heart of a poor unknown actor on TV, it becomes a little difficult to hear God's voice in your life. It's hard enough for most of us at the best of times to know what God's plans are and what he wants from us, but when we fill our lives with everything that is against what He is for, we end up hearing nothing. Get rid of the clutter, be different and allow God to transform your thoughts by staying away from potentially negative distractions.

Matthew 12:35 – *'Good people bring good things out of the good stored up in them, and evil people bring evil things out of the evil stored up in them'*
What do you have stored inside you? The reality is that what is inside you is only what you have already put there. If it's images of sex, violence, immorality and horror, then that is all you have to bring out. Be careful about what you soak up, because Jesus says that's what makes you YOU, and one day the world will see the real YOU on display by the good or evil stored up finally coming to the surface!!!

Listening point

There is something just so cool about being able to settle down and watch a really good movie, read an excellent book, listen to the latest release, or scan a juicy magazine. It's relaxing, it's enjoyable, it's stimulating and it's slacking at its very best! I believe each of these things are just how God wants it to be for us – if it's pleasurable then biologically it can only be good for us!

But like many questions in life, this is not a clear-cut issue. Think about it for a moment: you're watching TV at home with your parents and an unexpected and highly explicit sex scene comes on – do you sit there hoping it will finish quickly, switch to another channel, or indulge in the programme without giving it a second thought? If your friends were there – would you react in the same way? How about if you were alone? Here's another scenario: you're reading the 'problem page' of a magazine, when you realize your dad is looking over your shoulder – do you stop, put it down, or just carry on? If the point still hasn't hit home, how about this? You've just bought a new CD and as your mum drives you home, you try it out in the car. She listens to the lyrics. One of the songs starts to describe bi-sexual relationships. Do you die inside and hope the lyrics won't be too clear, do you just say how you like the tune, or do you turn it off? For most of us, our parents set the standard for what is acceptable and not acceptable. Yet in many cases we disregarded or ignore those standards when our parents are absent. It's like a person driving a car – speeding is fine until you spot a police car hiding behind a bush somewhere. Then you slow down and obey the law – you may not like it, but for that moment you're going to obey. Why bother? Because you don't want to get a ridiculous fine and face having points on your licence. In the presence of your parents or some other person you look up to, you don't want to rock the boat or have them think you are a pervert for watching anything more gripping than *Mary Poppins* or *The Sound of Music!* Most teenagers don't think twice about what they watch, read, or listen to when parents or other people they respect are absent. 'What I enjoy is down to the sort of person I am. It's my freedom of choice and expression – after all, if it's pleasurable then it can only be biologically good for me'. Do you think that's right?

Every now and then something extremely sick happens in our society: a child kills a toddler in a horrible way, or a teenager walks into a school with a knife or gun and blows away a few classmates. Everyone is shocked and disgusted. These are things nobody can understand. But actually this kind of behaviour shouldn't come as much of a surprise to anyone, in fact we should be relieved it doesn't happen more often. You may think that's going a bit too far. But actually it's not. Everyone is impressionable to some extent, at a conscious or subconscious level. The advertising industry knows this all too well, and uses techniques which they know people will respond to. One such technique even uses those controversial subliminal messages. These come and go, on a screen or CD player, in a fraction of a second, so that are not noticed consciously and yet part of your brain has picked up the message and may act on it.

Every time you see a film that has blood and guts flying everywhere, you are exposed to a level of violence and over a period of time you become less shocked by such scenes – your ideas about what is acceptable and unacceptable begin to change. Romantic novels that have sex scenes build up in you, over time, the impression that the standards shown in those books are acceptable. You may not believe this, but it has been tried and tested – the fact is that we are extremely impressionable people, particularly responsive to what we see and hear. The usual reason for premeditated peer killing by children or teenagers is the type of media influence they have surrounded themselves with. Often the actual murder itself is a copy of one in a film or story they were impressed by. Obviously, I'm not saying that because you have seen an 18-rated film you are doomed to wipe out your classmates, but what I am saying is that your mind has registered and absorbed an activity which could influence your attitudes in a negative way, at a later date.

Ebun and his friends took out a video which frightened the life out of them, to the point that they didn't even want to leave the house or go to sleep until it was light. These were tough masculine teenagers who until that movie had no problems walking anywhere in the middle of the night. Could that have been you? I remember as a teenager watching films that terrified me. Only later did I realize that some of the feelings I had and various social behaviours I had developed were direct results of certain horror movies that had lodged deep down in my mind. Don't forget, even when you are asleep, your mind never shuts off – it's continually working, thinking, and analyzing issues. Your dreams can be an indicator of that.

So where is this all going? Must we restrict ourselves to watching Disney, reading the *Chronicles of Narnia*, and listening to choir music only? Where is the fun and the freedom of expression and learning in that? The point I'm making is simply this: you begin your life with a blank piece of paper with nothing on it at all. For many people in this world, their sheet is marked by what they happen to see and by what others show them or force upon them. Choose carefully how you allow your paper to be marked because, without a shadow of a doubt, it changes you. Being a Christian is bound to be tough – doing what's right often doesn't come easily. So don't make it more difficult by indulging yourself in horrible or sexually corrupt images that you would never have seen or thought of, or by listening to music with anti-Christian ideas being played over and over again, or by playing games that make 18-rated violent films look like Sunday School material. If we want to be like Jesus then we need to surround ourselves with positive influences, as Philippians 4:8 reminds us 'whatever is true, whatever is noble, whatever is right, whatever is pure, whatever is lovely, whatever is admirable – if anything is excellent or praiseworthy – think about such things'. If we don't, then as Paul says in Romans 12, we will never be able to renew our minds. The end result is that the harvest of our lives will be whatever we have stored up in our minds (Matthew 12:35).

The choice is yours. You can decide what you feed (or harm) your mind on just as you can choose the type of food you choose to feed your body. The Bible tells us not to live like 'the world' teaches, but it doesn't forget that you are actually still living in the world. It's important that you don't cut yourself off from your culture or your friends, but it's equally important that you feed your mind and soul on wholesome food. It's down to you alone to decide what you watch, read, and listen to. I want to encourage you to first check out what kind of relaxation you're going to indulge in. You have the right to be responsible for your own choice and decisions – so make the right ones!

Radical Action Guide

Before you watch a film, read a book, browse the Internet, play on the PC/console, or listen to music, make the following decisions:

1. To have a preset standard that you choose not to go beyond, e.g. no sex or nudity scenes or no continual swearing.
2. To research what you are about to take pleasure from, e.g. read the reviews, the label and any descriptions you can find.
3. To ask the question throughout 'Would I be happy for my parents to be watching, reading, or listening to this with me?' If they would, then ask if you would be happy for Jesus to be sitting next to you?
4. Ask before you begin 'Is this 'pure, good and noble' for my mind and soul?'
5. Finally, ask yourself, 'will this in anyway distract me from my ultimate goal of drawing closer to Jesus?'

Video/Media

In what way do you think the 4 forms of media listed below affect each of the areas of your life both positively and negatively?

Physical

Mental

Social

Spiritual

1. Video/T.V./Cinema
2. Books/Magazines
3. Music
4. Internet/Games

From what you have read and the negative observations you have made about each of the 4 areas, where do you see the biggest need for change in your life, and how do you propose to do it?

Think it through...

General Notes...

Encouraged by...

discouraged by...

I need to Change...

EVALUATE

✓ Get it RIGHT!

Witnessing

The big issue

The speaker had come to the end of her talk; the atmosphere was electric. Two hundred teenagers were packed into the hall, the lights were low, and the band took up their places again. The music faded and she made her appeal 'You've heard the message tonight. God is calling each of us to be His witness, to shine with his light and to be his ambassador to the world ...' There wasn't a person not listening to her every word.

'Tonight,' she said, 'I want to set you a very special challenge. I want you to stand up in your place right now if you will speak to at least one of your friends this week who doesn't know Jesus. I want you to share his love with them and sow the seed of God's word in their lives!' The music continued to play and even before she had finished speaking people were standing up. Tim had been just as touched as anyone by the message, but he was a complete introvert. The thought of standing up in front of all these people was just too much for him – never mind speaking to a friend who probably thought he was a bit odd on the Jesus thing anyway. Within a couple of minutes the entire room had stood up, except Tim. He felt pressurised for not having stood up, and before he applied his brains he was up on his feet.

'Each of you who is standing has made a pledge before me and before God that you will speak to one person at least ... before the week is out!' Tim left the hall that night feeling uptight because he had agreed to do something he just couldn't do. He was terrified. 'It's OK if you're confident and outgoing!' he thought to himself. The days went by. Every lunch time he had the opportunity to talk to his college friends, on the way home he walked back with a classmate, and twice a week he went out to the skate boarders' park where there were people he knew. Each time, however, he just couldn't get round to saying anything. It was so unnatural and he was so bad at being natural. He didn't make use of these opportunities and by the end of the week he conceded defeat. He hadn't talked to anybody about Jesus. He had failed in his promise.

Talking point

- Do you think Tim was right to feel guilty? Explain your reasons.
- Do you think it was fair for Tim to have felt the pressure at the meeting he attended? Why do you think so?
- What do you think being a witness actually means?
- Do you find evangelism easy?
- Have you ever been involved in evangelism either with your friends or at organized events? How did you feel about it?
- In what ways could the following people share their faith, given their very different character?

    Quiet, shy, insecure, introvert

    Outgoing, confident, secure

    Extrovert, very confident, loud

- Do you enjoy sharing your faith?

- Do you find doing so natural or completely unnatural?

Bible point

We share our faith by example.
'Everyone will know you are my disciples, if you love one another' John 13:35.

We share our faith by both our words and also our actions.
'As you go, preach this message: "The kingdom of heaven is near". Heal the sick, raise the dead, cleanse those who have leprosy, drive out demons. Freely you have received, freely give' Matthew 10:7,8.

The Holy Spirit helps us to share our faith.
'But you will receive power when the Holy Spirit comes on you; and you will be my witnesses in Jerusalem, and in all Judea and Samaria, and to the ends of the earth' Acts 1:8.

We share our faith out of enthusiasm.
'Then they said to each other, "We're not doing right. This is a day of good news and we are keeping it to ourselves. If we wait until daylight, punishment will overtake us. Let's go at once and report this to the royal palace" 2 Kings 7:9.

Listening point

The doorbell rings ... the dog's going crazy. 'Just a minute!' you scream, half strangling the dog and pulling her into another room where you can close the door. After that, you shake yourself down, trying to get the hair off that now covers you like a mohair coat. 'Yeah?' you grunt at two odd looking people as you open the front door. 'What do you want?' They must be either salesmen or religious dudes. 'We are from the Church of ... ' Before they finish, you head back to the room where, behind the door, the dog is eating the furniture. Without any explanation, you give the 'Church of ...' (whatever), a little smile, and then open the door wide. The dog, smelling its prey, shoots past you and heads for the guys who are now running up the drive. Probably you have never actually been so cruel as to do that, but I bet you have felt like it, especially after three hours standing at the door, desperate for the loo, and not able to get a word in because the super-Christian evangelist hasn't even stopped to ask if you are a Christian. At times like that you may have wondered, 'Is this evangelism lark really necessary and does it do any good?'

Just before Jesus left his disciples he said, 'All authority in heaven and on earth has been given to me. Therefore go and make disciples of all nations ... ' (Matthew 28:18–19). He also said, 'As the Father has sent me, I am sending you'. (John 20:21). On another occasion he said, 'Freely you have received, freely give' (Matthew 10:8). It seems clear that Jesus wants us to get involved in telling the world about him. But how do we do it in a way that won't embarrass the pants off us – and our friends? Singing 'He's got the whole world in his hands' in the middle of town is not going to get you the award for being the coolest guy or girl in your school, college, or workplace. Knocking on people's doors and giving them a piece of paper that says, 'Receive Jesus or you will go to hell', isn't going to make you any friends. Nor is chasing people down the street until they eventually give in and then blasting them with Bible verses – that could easily land you a night in prison for harassment. I'm not knocking any of these kind of things, but they need to be done by people who are very gifted at doing it (and there are great organizations that offer training) otherwise it looks terrible at the very best and isn't what you'd call a great witness for Jesus. Most of us struggle even to tell people we are Christians and go to church. So when it comes to actually telling them about Jesus that's an almost impossible task. It was for Tim, and it probably is for you. Yet it doesn't need to be …

There were two people who met Jesus (although they didn't know it at the time) and they were so excited with the conversation that their hearts were 'burning within them' (Luke 24.32). Imagine that! Does your heart sometimes burn with excitement? If you followed me around you would quickly realize that I've far from cracked the Christian thing. My prayer times aren't like Pentecost every morning and my Bible studies don't always result in scales falling from my eyes as happened to Paul, when his life was dramatically changed. But just every now and then, I really 'get it'. I mean, I realize what being a Christian is all about and it blows me away. That is what people need to see. They can do without the boring and unexciting times in my life, when I've pulled the plug out of the power socket. People want to see the impact of electricity, not the object lying motionless. People want to see the impact of Jesus in you and what that actually means! Be sure to be plugged in and switched on …

Be relevant, don't talk religious nonsense – your mates most likely don't care about the flames of hell, but they do care about what kind of friend you are! They care about how you act, and live your life. If you don't smoke, swear, sleep around, gossip or get drunk, but you still know how to have a laugh and have fun, they will notice, because people will be watching every move you make! You are something new, something different. Soon you will get your opportunity when they ask you, 'how come you are so different?'

Don't shove Jesus at them as if you are hitting them over the head with a spade. Take your time; gently give things away. 'Yeah, I go to church!' or, 'Sure, being a Christian is far more exciting than anything else I've come across'. Give them bite-size information – that way you leave them a little bit more curious about who you are, and frustrated because they haven't been able to label you as a certified religious nut. The time will come when they want hard and fast answers, perhaps also when they need help and you can offer to pray for them or give them advice based on the Bible. One day you will reap what you have sown, in other words you will have friends who became Christians because you were the best example they had ever seen.

If that's what a witness is, if that is what Paul meant when he said that we are Christ's ambassadors (2 Corinthians 5:20) then Tim had no reason to feel guilty, and no more should you. Witnessing isn't easy, but it can be cringe-free and a lot of fun. Make it natural and you will see the results! Sure, you may want to get involved in formal outreach events (I would encourage you to because I believe in them). If they are done well they can have a big impact, as well as increasing your own faith. But in day-to-day living, being a witness doesn't mean you have to preach off a table in the common room at school or college or the coffee room at work. It simply means you have to be you, a great example of Jesus!

Radical Action Guide

1. Be enthusiastic about Jesus in your life (don't look as if you're dead miserable, but don't act like someone you're not – be real!)
2. Be relevant (scratch where people itch).
3. Keep off the religious hard stuff and be an example by how you live rather than by what you say.
4. Hand out bite-size information. Stop yourself from preaching and give them only the dose they need (too much can kill!).
5. Take the opportunity that comes your way, however it may come – such as praying for someone, giving a hug, being a shoulder to cry on, or being willing to help someone out with no strings attached.
6. Enjoy being you, and enjoy their curiosity about you!
7. When they are ready, reel them in – take them to church, or challenge them about where they are at or what they need.

What kind of witness am I

Which of the two are you most comfortable in doing when it comes to sharing your faith? Do you tend to be more comfortable in a public setting such as organised events or outreach, or are you more private and tend to get alongside people and be more relational in your approach?

Once you have decided which is most like you, then take a moment and answer <u>HOW</u> each of the 3 catagories of Public or Private evangelism best reflects your activities of witness.

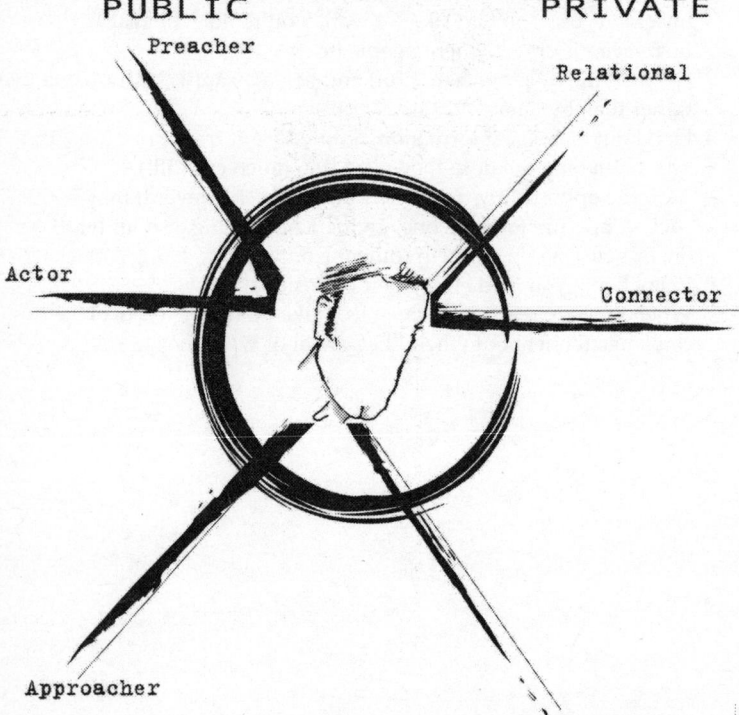

PUBLIC   PRIVATE

Preacher   Relational

Actor   Connector

Approacher

                        Being Approachable

# Think it through...

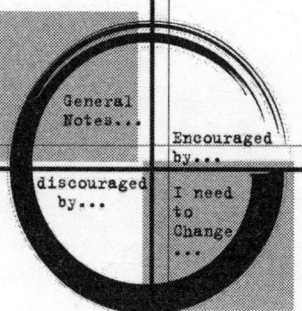

General Notes...
Encouraged by...
discouraged by...
I need to Change...

EVALUATE

✓ Get it RIGHT!

eXcellent worship!

The big issue

The church was completely packed with over 450 young people from 38 of the city's youth groups. Taking place once a month, this was generally agreed to be the most exciting event for the young people's groups to go to. The atmosphere was electric.

Adrian loved it: no preacher, no drama, just straight worship with breaks for prayer and the occasional testimony. 'Awesome' was about the only word he could think of to describe the evening. Anyone watching him could see he was totally absorbed with the event. He sang and prayed with a deep intensity, eyes closed, fists clenched, and when it came to testimony time he would be at the front of the queue for the microphone to tell of what God had done or said to him that night.

Yet Debbie, Adrian's youth leader was a little concerned by his behaviour. Something didn't quite add up: sure he acted like the most spiritual guy in the building, but his behaviour afterwards in the minibus and week by week at the youth fellowship was anything but spiritual. He swore, he was rude, he smoked, and occasionally he came to the group drunk. Debbie didn't have much experience as a youth leader – although she loved working with teenagers she had to admit she was fairly new at it, so she was more confused by Adrian rather than annoyed. Perhaps this could be acceptable for Christian teenagers. Acceptable or not she later decided, after catching him stabbing his knife into the mini bus seats that enough was enough. So she arranged to meet Adrian and confronted him with the double standards she had been seeing. 'Relax woman!' he replied jokingly, 'God is cool you know, you should take a dose of his stuff!' One thing was for sure, he was convinced about what he was saying and certainly couldn't see the double standard that his youth leader was gently hinting at. Debbie was lost for words and in defeat replied 'Ok Adrian, whatever!'

Talking point

- Was Adrian right – did Debbie need to relax a little and chill out, or do you think Debbie had a fair point?

- Adrian claimed that God did and said things to him throughout the evening; do you think God can be that close if we are holy in a meeting and unholy outside of it?

- Can you relate in any way to Adrian? You may not behave like him, but have you experience of entering into worship at church or an event, only to find you were just as bad at getting it right with God after the meeting as you were before the meeting?

- What are some of the things you really struggle with in your Christian life?

- What would you have said to Adrian had you been his youth leader?

- What do you think is the meaning of worship?

Bible point

Exodus 3:5 – 'Do not come any closer,' God said. "Take off your sandals, for the place where you are standing is holy ground."
Worship is encountering the living God. It's not about singing the latest songs, or having a band to jazz things up a bit (though I think that's great). However if singing songs and hymns leads you to him then it is a form of worship but we need to realize it isn't the only form of worship! God is holy (set apart from anyone or anything else) and also pure, and that means we should not just rush into worship by being super casual. Occasionally you may hear someone say, 'Jesus and I talked this morning, he's cool and now I'm cool!' Be careful how you worship God. Moses took off his shoes out of respect because he was on special ground (in the presence of God). It doesn't mean you should do the same, but it does mean you should hold a great respect for who God is.

Psalm 81:1-3 –'Sing for joy to God our strength; shout aloud to the God of Jacob! Begin the music, strike the tambourine, play the melodious harp and lyre. Sound the ram's horn at the New Moon, and when the moon is full, on the day of our feast.'

The psalm encourages us to worship God with songs and music. Singing is a wonderful way to express how we feel about God. Someone once said that singing is praying twice over. But the psalmist also draws our attention to the importance of special days for worshipping God. For us several thousand years later those days include Sundays, Easter, and Christmas. It is important to set whole days aside just to remember what God has done, but it is even more important to spend time with God every day. Be sure to worship him each day of your life, because he gives you each day to enable you to do that.

Romans 12:1 – *'I urge you, brothers and sisters, in view of God's mercy, to offer your bodies as living sacrifices, holy and pleasing to God – this is your spiritual act of worship.'*
Worship isn't just what you say, sing or read, it's much greater than that. God asks us to worship him with our lives. He asks us to be people who are different from anyone else simply because he is different, and by doing that we give great joy to him. By not swearing, getting drunk, lying, being negative, or gossiping you are showing the world there is something different with you, rest assured you are worshipping God even if you may not have prayed, sung, or read your Bible that day!

Listening point

You may not realize it but you are probably a great worshipper. 'I am?' you're thinking. Sure you are, we are all good at it. When David Beckham (or whoever you may rate), scores the most amazing goal and you say, 'He's fantastic' or you go to watch a film because it has Jennifer Lopez in it or some hot-shot actor and you drool the whole way through it, you are actually worshipping. When your head turns in the street to catch another glance of a shapely babe or fox passing by, and you are secretly dying inside because he or she is just too gorgeous, yep, it's worship! Sounds ridiculous doesn't it? 'I'm appreciating, but certainly not worshipping', you're thinking. Well let's see ... Without getting into the heavies of an English lesson, the word worship comes from an Anglo-Saxon word 'worth-ship'. Worship is giving worth or value to something or someone by what you say or do. So when you say your date is the hottest thing since the beginning of time you are giving worth to your boy or girlfriend and in a sense offering worship!

So when the Bible encourages us to worship God it doesn't mean 'Sing a bunch of songs in church for half an hour and that's your bit over and done with'. It means stop and think of just how wonderful God is. The God who created the world in a whisper, who has neither a beginning nor an end, has no limits of power or abilities, knows the very thought you are having right now, and decided at the exact moment he thought about making a place called earth that he would create you! Does he have much worth in your eyes, is he important? The answer you give is not proven here and now by a simple 'yes' or 'no', its in your everyday activities. If God is worth something to you then you will naturally show it by the way you live your life, the way and time you give to pray each day, how eager you are to read the Bible and books about him, how you spend your money, and where your thoughts are generally directed. What we give most of our free time and energy to is what we usually value the most! If we give it to computer games, music, going out with our friends, earning money, then that's where our values can be found. How much you worship God in any one week is based upon how much worth and value you give him in that one week.

Please don't miss the point and start feeling guilty because you clearly don't value him enough, don't feel claustrophobic as you imagine that worshipping God really means joining a monastery and donating every moment to him. That is not the message here. The real core message is this – that worshipping God is not a one-off event or a style of song or prayer (sure they add to it), but worshipping God is giving God value and we do that by our everyday actions! You can do it so many ways. If you want to smash someone on the nose, curse a jerk, or gossip about someone's most embarrassing secret, but you don't, because you know that's not what Christians should do, then you've got it, that's worship. You 'gave value' to God by changing your attitude. In other words, God mattered enough to you that you held off doing something negative. Kicking a ball around and playing on the computer is absolutely great if you want to have time to relax and chill out (God wants us to have fun and enjoy life). You're honouring God by looking after yourself (he gave you your body, don't forget). It's wrong though if you don't do your house chores, ignore your parents or dump your homework on the side so it collects dust. You're not giving worth to him because somewhere along the way you are not giving worth to somebody else. In many different ways the Bible tells us to obey others and put others before ourselves. And if you disobey the Bible, that sure isn't an act of worship. When you turn on the TV and find a steamy sex movie, but turn it over straight away – great, you just paid worth to God. You know the Bible tells us not to be lustful (steamy movies can make you pretty lustful) so out of respect for him you turn it over. Are you getting it yet? That's why Paul tells these Roman Christians to offer their bodies to God, holy and pleasing, as an act of worship. He didn't say, 'Give God your worship today by a minimum 15 minutes of prayer' – sure we should pray, because we need to nurture our relationship with him. But if we really want to please him, if we really want to say 'God you are great and worthy of my praise!' then don't just say it or sing it but do it with each decision you take!

Adrian was missing the whole point of worship. He thought it was just an experience to be had in singing and praying once a week or once a month, but worship is daily, hourly, moment by moment. You can tell your girlfriend or boyfriend you love them, you can express it in a kiss, but if you do things to hurt them or things they don't want you to do it isn't love, just words and feelings! Jesus said 'God is spirit, and his worshippers must worship in spirit and in truth'. (John 4:24). What he meant was simply this, if we want to worship God we should do it from the very core of our being, our hearts should be passionate about him, deeply in love with him, like the intensity of a flame burning within. With that kind of love, you can be sure your actions will prove again and again that your worship goes way beyond words and songs right to the point where we are being changed to be more like Jesus in our mind, body, social life and spirit!

Radical Action Guide

1. Worship God by being sure you encounter him daily (you may not feel or sense him, but your words and actions can certainly draw him close to you).
2. Worship God by asking him to control your thoughts, words, and activities.
3. Worship God by giving him time each day in prayer and Bible reading.
4. Worship God by looking after yourself mentally, physically, socially, and spiritually.
5. Worship God by taking your place as part of God's body (the church) and worshipping alongside other people.

Worship
(Xylophone)

1
2
3
4
5

1
2
3
4
5

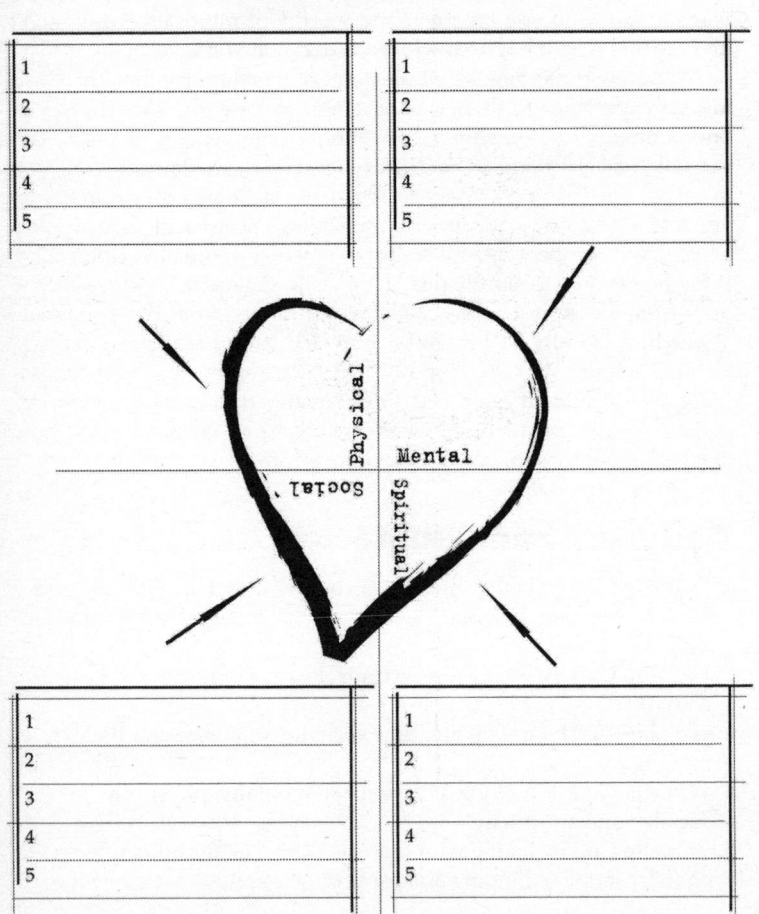

1
2
3
4
5

1
2
3
4
5

List 5 ways (in each of the boxes above) in which you worship God mentally, physically, socially and spiritually in any given week.

Think it through...

General Notes...
Encouraged by...
discouraged by...
I need to Change...

EVALUATE
✓ Get it RIGHT!

You've got it

The big issue

Kenya seemed an interesting choice for a family holiday. Not everyone was sold on it but it offers some of the world's greatest safari parks as well as the glorious African east coast beaches. Lars accepted the family deal, endured the endless jabs and tried to look at the positive aspects of the trip in spite of feeling that the rest of the family were a little too excited, his younger sister needed gagging, and his father should be shot for buying those ridiculous shorts that made him look like some nineteenth century missionary.

The holiday actually arrived and they landed at Nairobi airport. Lars' first experience of the locals came as he was walking out of the terminal to get a taxi. He was surrounded by children whom he thought were just happy to meet him; little did he realize at the time they were actually rifling through his pockets and backpack as he greeted them with a smile. The hotel was not quite what he had expected, and when he discovered that his wallet was missing, Lars was not best pleased with his introduction to Africa. In fact most of the time he just wanted to go home; the thought of being with his girlfriend at the pub was much more appealing. Not even the Masai Mara safari changed his feelings.

Then one day towards the very end of the holiday Lars, stuck in the back of a jeep and beginning to feel sick, suddenly sat bolt upright as the vehicle passed through a small community. What he had glimpsed vanished as quickly as he had seen it. A five or six-year-old semi-naked potbellied child was standing in the doorway In an old dilapidated house, or shack to be more precise, taking no notice of the swarms of flies around him. Lars had been unmoved by such images a thousand times before on the news and TV documentaries, but something in that split second hit deep.

As soon as Lars returned home he phoned the church youth pastor and told him he wanted to go back to Kenya over the coming summer holidays, this time with the rest of the youth group, to serve communities like those he had seen. His youth worker laughed and told him to get a good night's sleep!

Talking point

- Do you think Lars was being idealistic in wanting to go back with the youth group and help in the summer? Explain your reasons.
- What did Lars have to offer that would be helpful to an African community?
- Have you ever been moved by an experience and wanted to go (back) and help?
- Have you ever been on a short-term mission trip?
- If you could go anywhere in the world and serve people in any way, where would you choose to go, how might you serve and why would you go there?

    Where?

    How?

    Why?

- It was something Lars saw that inspired him to go back and help. God can lay a city or country on our heart in different ways. Has God laid some place on your heart? If so, how has he done it and what do you think might come of this?

Bible point

Christians are called to serve.
'So he [Jesus] got up from the meal, took off his outer clothing, and wrapped a towel around his waist. After that he poured water into a basin and began to

wash his disciples feet, drying them with the towel that was wrapped around him' John 13:4–5.

Christians are called to be selfless.
'If someone forces you to go one mile, go two miles. Give to the one who asks you, and do not turn away from the one who wants to borrow from you' Matthew 5:41–42.

Christians are called to love Jesus by loving others.
'Lord, when did we see you hungry and feed you, or thirsty and give you something to drink? When did we see you a stranger and invite you in, or needing clothes and clothe you? When did we see you sick and in prison and go to visit you?
'The King will reply, "I tell you the truth, whatever you did for one of the least of these brothers and sisters of mine, you did for me"' Matthew 25:37–40.

Listening point

As we sit and watch our TVs we see yet another disaster, another war, another famine, another flooding, another volcano erupting – there's always something happening. Somewhere in this world, perhaps not across the street or even in this continent, but someone is without a home, without food, fresh water, or clothes. The images flash across our screens but we have become so used to seeing people struggling to survive that we continue to enjoy our fish and chips, feeling little or no concern. But though you may not feel anything, rest assured God does – for every person in need he cries out, 'Who will love and help this child of mine?' You may not be catapulted out of bed one night by his audible voice; you may not see his question written across the sky; but you can be sure the next time you see a desperate picture of human need, God is asking, 'Who will help?'

Christianity was born when Jesus came and died on a cross two thousand years or so ago to rescue humankind from disaster. Ever since then Christians have gone all over the world showing God's love in practical ways. A starving child isn't ready to be told about Jesus dying on the cross – they need to be shown it by being fed; a sick mother needs to be shown it by being able to get hospital treatment, knowing her children are being taken care of; a family whose house has fallen down needs a new one; and the orphan who has lost both parents needs long-term security. Sure, the world needs preachers and evangelists but it also needs lovers and servers. When Christians get their hands dirty and work with suffering people, helping to change their world, something happens at a cosmic level, and in this world people sit up and begin to watch. When love like this is on offer, who needs to preach? The message is in the act!

'Sounds good', you may be thinking, 'but what has this got to do with me?' Perhaps you are a student, with hardly any money; perhaps you have no formal qualifications yet, no fully developed skill or trade to offer and you have a full schedule. What on earth can someone like you offer those in need? In all likelihood you have much to offer, but here are three basic suggestions for you to consider the next time you are moved by images of people in desperate need.

Radical Action Guide

1. *Pray* – Start by collecting as much information as you can on the subject, facts, situations, conditions, and needs. With the information and pictures you have acquired from the TV, papers, and magazines, either on your own, with a friend, or in your church youth group, take time to pray. Bring the needs you have listed to God and ask him to respond to your requests. Remember Jesus' story about the persistent widow (Luke 18). The difference here is God wants to answer your prayers while the judge in the story merely gave in under pressure …

2. *Inform* – Write to mission agencies asking what they are doing in that location of the world or how they are helping in that particular crisis. Ask what their needs are at present in trying to help with relief or social concern. Again collect information from the TV and papers and then begin to distribute this information within your community. Ask your youth leader whether the youth group can take this up as a fundraising project and creatively come up with ways to help financially those involved in the latest crisis.

3. *Go* – Whether you are fourteen or twenty-one, student or unemployed, skilled or unskilled, you have much to offer. There are dozens of short term missions from just ten days to one year where you could actually serve those in need first hand. You could see troubles for yourself and be moved beyond belief just like Lars was. What skills or diplomas do you need to saw a piece of wood, dig, push a wheelbarrow, hold and nurse a baby, play with underprivileged kids, cook a bowl of rice? The answer is none, and even if you did you could learn on the spot. Travelling with a mission is not always cheap, you will certainly need to find funding. However, if God's calling you and you want to go enough, you will find it somehow. The best place to start is by finding the organization you wish to go with and then approach your minister or youth pastor.

Make a difference by committing yourself to doing one or more of the above. Somewhere, at some point, someone in this world will be grateful for what you did; neither you nor they may ever know exactly who it was, but rest assured God does! And on the day you meet your Maker he will turn to you and say, 'Well done, good and faithful servant, you have been faithful with a few things ... come and share in your master's happiness!' (Matthew 25:21).

You can't change the whole world, you can't respond to every need, but if you start on one thing and other believers do the same, then before you know it our world will be a very different place. Play your part and remember – 'what you did for one of the least of these brothers and sisters of *Jesus*, you did for *him*!' (Matthew 25:40).

You've got it
(Service)

Which of these areas do you think God has placed on your heart?	Write the location
Africa	
Asia	
Europe	
Australia	
America	

What can you offer? (Gifts/Resources)

Which of these 3 ways mentioned are you most likely to help serve with	Explain in detail how
Pray	
Inform	
Go	

In what other ways can you help?

Think it through...

General Notes...	Encouraged by...
discouraged by...	I need to Change...

EVALUATE

✓ Get it RIGHT!

Zits, weight ...and all that stuff

The big issue

Her scars were not on the outside – they were too deep for anyone ever to see or reach. If you ever got close then Becky Griffin would react. The last time she reacted was at home over the meal table when her father commented that she had put on a few pounds lately. Becky didn't say anything; she just got up out of her chair and left the house. She was sixteen years old at the time, her final exams were coming up, but when she walked out of the house she did so for good. Her family and friends had not seen Becky for the last three years. There hadn't been a day in which her father had stopped wishing he had never opened his mouth. Her mother had been so shocked and traumatized that she had been in and out of a psychiatric hospital. Their only prayer had been that wherever Becky was she would be safe and that she was doing OK. They clung to the memories of their daughter, remembering her as a child, all the great things they did together, how much she had made them happy when she laughed, sad when she cried. She was the most precious thing in their lives and she had gone after one dumb remark.

One night the phone went. Mr Griffin answered and the conversation soon caught his wife's attention. After he had finished he put the phone down, half smiling, half crying, and said, 'They have found her, she's OK. But…' and he paused, 'they found her walking the streets. They've arrested her for prostitution. She doesn't have money to pay the bail'. Then tears began to fall as husband and wife embraced. After a few moments they got themselves together and drove across the city. After they had gone through the paper work at the police station and handed over the money, the moment came when they could finally see Becky again. She was now nineteen. They had expected to see changes but not so many. She had lost so much weight, her clothes were short and revealing, her hair had changed, and she seemed to have pierced almost every available site.

Becky was clearly feeling awkward and her parents were numbed. Finally her father approached her looked into her eyes and with tears rolling down his face, whispered, 'Becky, I'm so sorry for what I've done to you; you will never know how much I regret what I said that night to my little girl'. Becky said nothing but her eyes never left him. 'You mean everything to me,' he said, 'to know you're alive and well is all I have prayed for since you left. If you never speak to me again, two things will not change. I will always be so glad to have seen you and to see you are well. The other thing is – I will always love you.'

Becky didn't look at him. She turned her head towards the door and asked the police officer 'Am I free to go?' The officer nodded and Becky headed towards the door. When she reached it she turned and looked at her father. 'Daddy, all my life people have made fun of me and hurt me. But it never mattered because I thought my daddy loved me no matter what, but the day you said what you did that hurt more than all the things anyone else had ever said.' With that she turned and walked out.

Mr and Mrs Griffin went home grieving. This had been the most painful day of their lives – the day they first found their daughter and then lost her again.

Three long months passed and then there was a knock at the door. Mr Griffin found himself face to face with his daughter again. She had just one question for him. 'Daddy, did you really mean it when you said you were sorry?' Without any hesitation he whispered to her, 'I've never been more sorry about anything in my life.' He held out his hands and the two hugged.

Talking point

- What, if anything, shocks you about this story?
- What can you relate with most in this story?
- What kind of pain was Becky feeling?
- Becky was very sensitive about her appearance; do you ever feel concerned about how you look to others? Can you explain why you do/don't feel this way?
- Becky's dad was the one person who could hurt her more than anyone else, with just a casual or flippant remark. Whose opinion matters most to you?

- How do each of the following make you feel about your appearance?

    School friends

    Parents

    God

- How do you feel when:

    Wearing trendy clothes.

    Wearing expensive brand names.

    Wearing cheap clothes.

    Wearing old clothes.

- Does your appearance matter to you personally? Why does/doesn't it?

Bible point

Genesis 1:27 – *So God created human beings in his own image, in the image of God he created them; male and female he created them.*
Have you ever thought of yourself looking like God? Anyhow – what does God look like – good looking with all the latest clothes? 'Don't be ridiculous!' you reply. Quite right, too. God doesn't have a physical body, so how he looks and the clothes he wears is a totally 'off the wall' thought. The passage means we were created to be like him below the surface, in other words in character. God really cares about what you look like because he made you, but he cares much more about what

your character is like because he designed you to be just like him in that area!

1 Peter 3:3–4 – *'Your beauty should not come from outward appearance, such as braided hair and the wearing of gold jewellery and fine clothes. Instead, it should be that of your inner self, the unfading beauty of a gentle and quiet spirit, which is of great worth in God's sight'*

Braided hair and dripping with gold jewellery must have been the 'in' thing for women two thousand years ago. This may or may not repel you. The message here is, regardless of trend, don't settle for just looking good because there is more to you than how you look. You have a character and personality and that's what makes people like or dislike you.

Esther 1:11 – *'[The king's servants brought] before him Queen Vashti, wearing her royal crown, in order to display her beauty to the people and nobles, for she was lovely to look at'*

We might not all want to be like Queen Vashti – a pair of Levi's and a Gap shirt will do fine for us. Looking good is important to most of us, and that's not a bad thing. If God made us beautiful or handsome, we shouldn't do anything to hide that, but remember, God looks on the inside!

Listening point

Bleary-eyed, you climb out of bed. You feel like you've just completed ten rounds with the heavyweight boxing champion of the world. You catch sight of yourself in the bathroom mirror. 'Arrrrh!' you scream, your hair is terrible, sticking up and stiff with grease, but that's not the main problem. A shower will solve that. More serious is the blackhead neatly sitting between your left nostril and your cheek. Wiping the sleep out of your eyes, you realize to your dismay that the zit looks even bigger than before – it's so obvious, so repulsive, your dreams lie shattered, not a chance of ever getting to go out with the person you have been chasing for the whole of this term.

Ever been in a situation like that? Of course you have! Not even all the disasters in the world may seem to equal the personal tragedy of having a bad hair or zit day. How you look matters because it affects how you feel. If you look good then you usually feel good, if you look bad then you probably feel like trash. How we appear has a lot to do with our self-esteem. If we wear trendy clothes, are slim, and have an expensive hair cut then our self-esteem rises. If you are overweight, your clothes don't seem to fit or look good on you, and your haircut looks like the hair-dresser used a pudding bowl then your esteem is most likely at an all-time low.

Becky was tired of being made fun of because of her weight; people had made every possible joke about her size, she had been called many offensive names. Yet somehow she lived through it all because her value didn't come from her friends but from her dad. When her dad for a moment lost the plot so did Becky – her world was over. Everything everyone had ever said to her suddenly rang true. She was nothing special, a nobody, and overweight, so she bailed out of normal life. Seeking love she found love of a sort and even got paid. It's a terrible story! But Becky isn't alone: the streets of our big cities are filled with teenage prostitutes who have been told too many lies; the mortuaries receive too many young people who take their lives because they have a poor image of themselves and think others despise them. The wards of children's hospitals are littered with people who are either anorexic or bulimic, so obsessed by how they think they appear that they punish their bodies. Most of us don't react in such an obvious way; we suffer in silence convinced that we are not good-looking, perhaps too podgy, with a wardrobe full of seconds, and a relative who insists on cutting our hair rather than letting us go to a professional. The wounds of self-consciousness are deep. But you know what, by and large, it's one big horrible lie!

People who are skinny, attractive and own a wardrobe their friends would die for are just as unhappy, just as deeply scarred and just as low in self-esteem as the next person. They might not be targeted with the jokes others receive, or feel almost every TV programme pressuring them to be something they are not, but in reality most people in this world wish they could be someone else, and are highly dissatisfied with the way they actually are! But what really matters is not how you look, or even how good you are at doing this or that – it's simply who you are. Around 90-95 per cent of the time we are attracted to other people by their personalities, not how hot they are or how clever they may be but how nice, kind, warm, and generous they are. We've all met people whom you just want to drool over because of their looks but who turn out to have personalities as cold as the Arctic, and their friends may be similar. The people with the most friends and happiest marriages later on in life are neither the hunks nor the Einsteins but the people with warm personalities. When Peter in his letter said to forget the 'braided hair and the gold' he wasn't saying appearances didn't matter, but he was encouraging us to work on our personalities more because that is what people will find most attractive about us.

When Samuel was trying to choose a new king for Israel he was fooled by the appearance of Jesse's sons but God brought him back to reality by warning him, 'Do not consider his appearance or his height, for I have rejected him … the Lord looks at the heart' (1 Samuel 16:7). How you look is important because it does affect how you feel *towards* yourself, but it doesn't change deep down how you feel *about* yourself. God loves you because you are who you are. Some people will judge and love you or hate you because of the way you look, but those who really know you will love you because of the real you. They don't care what you look like. They just want *you*.

It's a sobering thought that some people spend more money on a haircut than it costs to keep a child in a hospital or an orphanage in Africa for a year. Some people spend more money rearranging their boobs than it would cost to feed an entire village in a Third World country for several years. People in the West are generally obsessed by looks and yet we still haven't learned that the sexiest, most attractive, and greatest 'feel-good' factor we can experience is from dealing kindly with another human being.

Becky gained all her confidence and strength from her ally (her dad), and when he failed her, she failed by opting out. We all need friends and supporters to keep our heads above water, to stop the scars spreading further and deeper, but the reality is that once in a while even those we trust will fail us. All except God; his love for you is never ending and is unlimited. It's not based on appearance, intellect, or achievement, it's based on acceptance. He loves you because he loves you; he loves you because you are his. No other reason than that. He may want you to do well in certain things, but if you fail that's not the end, because he loves you for who you are! Take time to look good and feel good, but remember it's who you are that really counts. Your looks, measurements, and clothes are not the ticket to success in relationships and life, it's the real you that attracts. And the real you is always deep below the surface of your skin. Be confident in life because you have good reason to be. You are loved and accepted by God simply because you are his, and others love you because of what a great person you are, irrespective of how fit and trendy you may or may not feel!

Radical Action Guide

1. Enjoy looking good.
2. Wear clothes that both feel comfortable and suit you.
3. Hang around the friends who make you feel good and not around people who always make you feel not attractive enough.
4. Go out of your way to make someone's day by what you say or do, rather than trying to turn a head and attract someone by what you wear.

5. Be yourself in everything you do from personality to appearance; don't let others dictate what you should be like.
6. Take your confidence from who you are, not how you look or appear.
7. Most important of all, remember God loves you simply because you are his child. What anyone else thinks about you is secondary. You matter and you are important; to God your appearance is irrelevant.

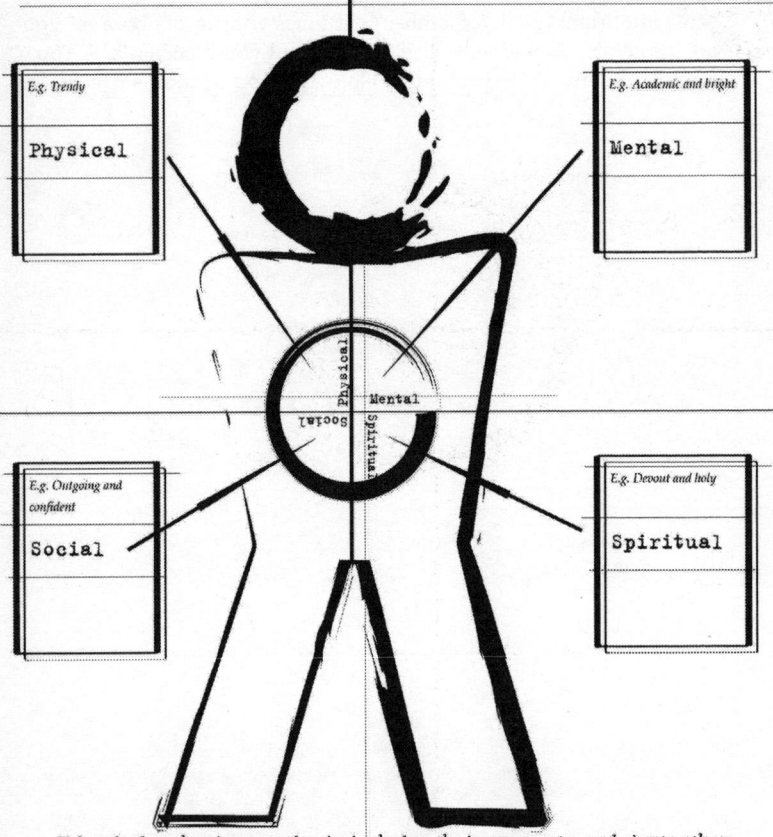

 # Think it through...

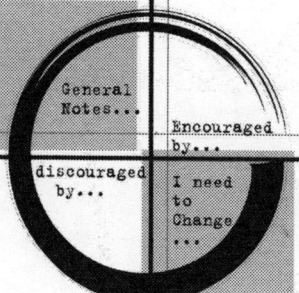

General Notes...
Encouraged by...
discouraged by...
I need to Change...

EVALUATE

✓ Get it RIGHT!